From the Field— Member Tips & Insights

North American Hunting Club
Minnetonka, Minnesota

From the Field—Member Tips & Insights

Printed in 2006.

Tom Carpenter *Creative Director*

Heather Koshiol *Book Development Coordinator*

Teresa Marrone *Editor*

David Rottinghaus *Illustrations*

BatScanner Productions, Inc. *Book Design and Production*

ISBN 1-58159-108-X
7 8 9 10 / 09 08 07 06
© 2000 North American Hunting Club

North American Hunting Club
12301 Whitewater Drive
Minnetonka, MN 55343
www.huntingclub.com

Photography

Photos accompanying each article were supplied by the NAHC Members who wrote each piece.

Cover Photo:
Donald M. Jones

Additional photography:
Mike Barlow—11
Lance Beeny—6 (bottom) 12, 23, 26, 56, 63, 82 (top), 110, 139 (bottom), 140
Tom Carpenter (NAHC)—4-5, 20, 133 (inset)
Beth Davidow, The Green Agency—65
Mike Faw—6 (top), 42, 138 (left),146
John R. Ford—47, 66 (top), 67 (bottom), 68, 74, 84
Dan Kennedy (NAHC)—51, 91, 95 (both), 105 (ATV tip), 106, 108, 115, 120 (book tip), 131, 133 (pack), 136
Rich Kirchner, The Green Agency—8, 118
Lance Krueger—120 (elk)
Bill Lindner—54, 122 (bottom right), 127
Teresa Marrone—123 (bottom), 135, 148-152
Stan Osolinski, The Green Agency—82 (bottom), 83 (top), 92, 101, 138 (bottom), 154
Greg Schweiters—105 (deer)
Dusan Smetana, The Green Agency—7 (bottom), 21
Tom Tietz—58
Bill Vaznis, The Green Agency—61
NAHC—124

Additional Illustrations:
Teresa Marrone—116-117, 129

Table of Contents

Introduction . . . . page 4

Strategies & Species. . . . . page 6

Ways with Weapons . . . . page 66

Equipment Essentials . . . . page 82

Outdoor Observations . . . . page 122

Final Flourishes . . . . page 138

Index. . . . . page 156

It doesn't matter how long you've been hunting. When you think you know everything there is to know, it's time to hang up your camo or blaze orange or canvas, put your rifle or shotgun or bow away for good, and retire to an easy chair. Because if you quit being excited about any hunting season, refuse to expand your knowledge of game, ignore opportunities to improve all your skills ... then you've lost the essence of what hunting is.

That's why this book, *From the Field—Member Tips & Insights,* is so important. Fellow members become the stars, sharing their real-life, from-the-field ideas, each of which will help you become an even better hunter. You'll find exciting stories along with gems of advice on hunting whitetails, turkeys, elk, mulies, pronghorns, bears, gamebirds, waterfowl and small game.

NAHC members had their pens busy to create this book, that's for sure. But they also used their cameras to take a lot of great photos, and those results are pictured here too.

You'll also find strategies and tips from a variety of great hunting writers associated with the North American Hunting Club: Out West columnist, book author and Bowhunting Advisory Council (BAC) member Bob Robb; Shock Therapy columnist and outfitter Jim Shockey; Bowhunting columnist and BAC member Chuck Adams; book author and turkey addict Glenn Sapir; Whitetails columnist Mark Kayser; book author Ron Spomer; book author and outfitter Jim Van Norman; and hunting and fishing club advisor Chris Winchester. Your editor shares a few items too. These ideas merely accent what the book features: member hunting tips and insights.

You'll glean hunting wisdom and knowledge from this book. More than anything else, it's like a late-night hunting camp session around the campfire or woodstove—great talk, great stories, and great ideas that will help you drag in a good deer, lug in a big gobbler, or have just about any other hunting success you can think of, tomorrow.

Tom Carpenter
Editor, North American Hunting Club Books

STRATEGIES & SPECIES

Nothing teaches better than experience, and in this chapter you'll learn from experiences shared by fellow NAHC Members. From still-hunting to stalking to stand-hunting, elk to pigs to whitetails, here's where you'll find strategies, techniques, tips and tricks for locating and hunting all sorts of North American wild game.

In addition to the knowledge your fellow NAHC Members shared, our panel of experts contributed tips and tricks written especially for this book.

Whether you read this chapter straight through or simply browse around, you'll find a wealth of knowledge that is sure to make you an even better hunter.

Better Your Hunting Skills

One of the best tips I can give you is to be patient. You can't rush the sunrise and you can't beat the sunset, so don't rush the day. Take a lunch and plan to stay all day, if you can. You need to be in the woods as much as possible. I know that most of us hunters have families and it's sometimes hard to get away. Why not take your family with you? Have a picnic, go for a drive in the evenings, pick berries or go fishing.

The next step is scouting, such as looking for antlers in your hunting area, rubs from past seasons, winter kills, scrapes, populations of animals in the area, tracks and trails, and sources for food and water.

Hunt the same area consistently. Don't hunt two days in one spot and three days in another, then back for two more days in the first. Stay in your first-choice area because sooner or later the animals will come around and give you a chance. Again, be patient and don't second-guess yourself; if you do, you might miss the chance of a lifetime.

I have very good luck when I walk instead of driving or road-hunting. You can drive and still fill your tags, but you won't see as many animals and probably not harvest as many either. Walking increases your chances of seeing more and bigger animals than you would if you were driving. Hunting season is only a short time out of the year, so try to walk as far and as much as you can because you rarely get a second chance. If you think about climbing up a hill or going another mile or two, do it … you never know when or where you'll see that trophy.

The best advice I can give is to

> *If you think about climbing up a hill or going another mile or two, do it … you never know when or where you'll see that trophy.*

spend time sitting, because most of my animals come from sitting. A place where the animals come to feed or drink is the best place to sit, in my book. If they don't come the first day, just be patient and keep repeating the process. If you know the animals are there, then you should know that sooner or later they will come around.

Curtis Deschamps
Colorado Springs, CO

FROM THE EXPERT'S NOTEBOOK

Play the Does and Cows ... by Ron Spomer

When hunting whitetails, elk, pronghorns or most other big game during the rut, take your cues from the females. A buck or bull in love is not going to abandon an estrus doe or cow, so if you can fool the girls, you'll get the boy-friend. For example, after watching a large herd of elk feed over a ridge into timber, my guide and I hurried over and cow called. A 6X7 satellite bull forced to the fringes of the main herd must have thought this a chance to steal a kiss. He turned back and walked right to us.

While slipping through a cattail slough in November, I jumped a truly huge whitetail buck. Too thick to shoot. But I stood quietly, watching, and soon saw him sneaking back. He came within 40 yards and I made several photographs before finally spooking a doe that had been lying between us. Another time I crested a hog back ridge to see a wide-racked whitetail 100 yards away staring straight at me. A plum thicket obscured all but his upper neck and head. Rather than shoot hastily, I eased up my Winchester, wrapped the sling around my arm, and took careful aim before parking a 165-grain Nosler in his neck. At the shot, a doe bounced from the thicket. I didn't know, but suspected, that was why an otherwise alert and wary buck hadn't run off as soon as he saw me approach.

Study bucks and bulls every chance you get in parks and even zoos to gain a better understanding of their body language and behaviors around estrus females. It'll pay off.

Walk and Talk Like the Animals

My son and I were hunting elk in Wyoming when we spotted a small group of elk about a thousand yards away. We started to stalk them, but quickly came across some antelope. We didn't want to spook the antelope for fear they would, in turn, spook the elk. There was no way to get to the elk with the wind direction and cover we had, other than to go past the antelope. There had been cattle grazing in the area, so my son started to bellow like a cow. The antelope started coming closer to us. We continued walking, and they continued to come closer. My son bellowed occasionally as we continued along, and they allowed us to walk right past them at 50 yards without spooking. We stalked within shooting distance of the elk, and I was able to take a 5X5 bull.

The lesson we learned is this: Make the sounds of animals around you, to avoid spooking other animals in the area.

Gordon Kragt
Holland, MI

Spike Camps: Improve Your Odds

It's a fact: Hunting pressure and human activities affect the outcome of most hunts. Even in Alaska, popular areas or those with high-density game populations become crowded during the hunting seasons. It's not uncommon to spend two hours in a floatplane only to land on a lake and find two or more camps already present. For long-time Alaskan hunters, as well as first-timers seeking to experience a true Alaskan big game hunt, this can be very discouraging.

I experienced these frustrations many times until I realized one common pattern: all the hunters at these other camps would start and end each day at base camp. This requires covering the same area day after day, hunt after hunt, camp after camp, until any big game animals were harvested or had left the area. How could I land in the same location after all of that and increase my odds for success?

When hunting game like moose, sheep, black or brown bears, mountain goats or caribou, your odds diminish rapidly in this situation. Let's face it: most hunters on foot travel no farther than two or three miles in any one direction from the security of their camp. Success ratios for these hunters can be pretty low; as an example, moose hunters in Alaska have a success ratio of 15 to 20 percent. Are you willing to accept these percentages, or would you like to increase your odds to 75 to 90 percent? Simple question, with a simple answer: spike camp!

If you think that hunting pressure along with planes, ATVs, boats and other vehicles don't affect big game activities and movements, then base camp is good enough for you. But if you are in for adventure, excitement and added challenge and would like to experience the true meaning of "hunting," then go to the woods … go to the mountains …

go where the animals are still in control. I think sheep and goat hunters are the biggest spike camp enthusiasts. Perhaps that's because spike camps are obviously necessary for the successful pursuit of these elusive animals.

In this new millennium, have we let the technical world control and restrict our hunting boundaries? Are we afraid to leave the security of our campers, boats and four-wheel-drive SUVs for the one true reason we go to the woods in the first place—the hunting experience? This phrase seems to have lost its luster as the years have turned young men with dreams of adventure and excitement into men of leisure and comfort. Will dependency on mechanical comforts rob your sons and daughters of their dreams of adventure and excitement, or is a night, or two, or three in the woods still in *your* future?

Here are some points to consider:
- Pack lightly but comfortably; remember, you are only a mile or two away from more supplies.
- Know the area in which you're hunting.
- Camp in a spot with good visibility.
- Choose a camping spot with access to fresh water, if possible.
- Keep a low profile; don't disturb the natural order of things.
- Allow enough time to pack out all your meat.

Mike O'Connor
Anchorage, AK

PHOTO ABOVE: *Mike O'Connor with his 63-inch bull moose at spike camp: "The moose woke us up at 1:00 a.m., and stuck around 'til daylight!"*

The Hidden Deer

It has been said that you learn from your mistakes. I sure hope so, because this mistake kept me from filling my buck tag. This could have happened to any deer hunter, and because of that we must all be aware of the hidden deer.

My story is about a mistake I made during my second season of hunting in Nebraska. I moved to the state the year prior, but had arrived too late to apply for a buck tag so I settled for a doe permit. On opening day, I was amazed when an 8-point buck walked within 20 yards of my stand. It stopped and snorted at me, pawed the ground and snorted some more. It was as though the buck knew I couldn't shoot! Later that day I shot a doe; but because of that 8-pointer staring me down, I was really excited for the next season to roll around.

The next year, my son and I spent a lot of time in that area in preparation for hunting. But just before deer season, an early snowfall devastated the area. Heavy, wet snow brought limbs to the ground and toppled full-grown trees. The area was in shambles. My son had lived in the area for several years, and suggested we go instead to a spot he had hunted in the past. With no time left to scout the area, we were destined to enter the woods with cold feet on opening day.

We arrived an hour before daybreak, and walked to the back side of a cornfield. My son headed to a spot he knew from previous years, while I decided to follow a series of runways. I saw lots of rubs, and sat at two different spots over the next six hours, but saw only squirrels and birds.

I decided to head in for something to eat. The spot I had been in for the last two hours was on a runway headed into a small field. I had heard about deer under pressure laying low in tall grass, so before getting up, I glassed the field. I didn't see anything but decided to walk around the field anyway. At the edge of the field, I found a nice rub, with a fresh scrape next to it. Suddenly I heard something behind me. I turned just in time to see a 6-point buck running across the field. I raised and sighted in as the deer was entering the woods on the other side of the field. I missed, and could only watch as the deer bounded into the woods.

After I collected my thoughts, I began to examine what had happened. Apparently this buck was laying under a low-hanging limb, watching his scrape. When I walked up, he waited until my back was turned before running out. I had never glassed the edge of the field as I figured there wasn't enough cover to hide a deer.

That day, I learned that deer can hide anywhere. It doesn't take much, so my advice is this: The next time you think no deer are around, think again. They might be hiding right next to you. Oh yes, my son got a 5-point that afternoon!

Clark B. Butler
Lakeland, FL

quick tip

Search Mode

A tactic I use to try to even the odds is what I call "search mode." I divide the terrain into three areas: close, medium and far. Close is out to 30 yards, medium is 30 to about 60 yards, and far is the horizon. I check each area from near to far, and then back. I use a good pair of binoculars, more for the light-gathering ability than anything, but it's surprising how much an antler looks like a branch at 40 yards. The best piece of advice I can give when you're searching like this is to take your time, and remember … the deer have all day and all night.

Frank Rostar
Charlevoix, MI

Patience and Persistence Pay Off

My fifth archery season ended up being my most rewarding season. Not only did I successfully take my streak-saving fifth pronghorn in five years, I also harvested the biggest I've ever shot. With 16-inch tall, 5-inch bases, and 6½-inch prongs, this may be the new Montana state record Pope and Young Club antelope. (I'm still searching for an official scorer.)

Antelope are my favorite animals to bowhunt. Don't get me wrong; my passion for mule deer and elk is extreme, but there are limits to how much quality archery hunting a person can have in one day for elk and mulies. Feeding habits, weather, and time of year give a bowhunter only a few solid hours of great elk or muley hunting each day.

Antelope, on the other hand, can be hunted all day long, regardless of the weather or time of year. Antelope don't have any predictable feeding pattern; they just venture around, exposing themselves to any decent pair of binoculars. Their best hiding area is out in the most open piece of ground they can find. Their vision is excellent, but other senses are somewhat lacking. Taking advantage of their weakness and using it against them is my art.

During archery season, most bowhunters try to take advantage of stands and blinds while others jump all over the rut by using a decoy. All of my success has come with the spot-and-stalk method.

I've learned to appreciate the hardcore hunting involved in spot-and-stalk. These few helpful hints will help guarantee your success and also help you have the most enjoyable hunt you've ever experienced.

Don't overhunt. If you find yourself walking until your feet hurt so badly you won't get out of bed the next day, you're overdoing it (or you're not watching

Antelope keep an eye out for each other, which makes it all the more difficult to get close enough for an archery shot.

for cactuses!). Pick out a good, high spot and glass, glass, glass. Try to let your eyes do more work than your feet. My goal is to gather all the information I need to stalk the antelope. I prefer stopping and setting up a plan of attack with the spotting scope, but that's not always possible.

After spotting an animal, plan your attack. I look for natural barriers like trees or big rocks to hide behind. Sometimes even tall sagebrush provides great concealment to crawl through.

Creeks and hills are always a major advantage. Not only are you hidden, you can relax and take time to think out your situation. Take plenty of time, too, and never make the mistake of skylining yourself. If you pop over the top of a hill instead of around it, you'll never get so much as within

quick tip

Out-Foxing a Fox

When using the spot-and-stalk method for red fox in open farm country, if you miss a shot and the fox did not see you, it pays to remain where you are and wait. Oftentimes the fox will return to the same general area where it was laying, giving you another shot opportunity. I have had fox run over a hill after a missed shot, only to come back and run right at me. Key to this method is that you must stalk to your shooting position without being detected. The fox, not realizing where the shot came from, will oftentimes come back to investigate.

Rob Harrison
Hudson, SD

rifle distance of any antelope in the county. Watch the wind, too. I know that's basic; but don't watch it primarily because of scent, watch it because of sound. Antelope don't have a great sense of smell, but they hear fairly well and the wind carries sound just that much farther. For two of my kills, I sneaked right up on the buck with the wind at my back, blowing right at my prey. Just move slowly and as quietly as possible. If you spend ample time spotting and planning out your stalk, you'll have pretty good odds.

Try to locate bucks that are off by themselves. Generally, the bigger bucks are alone, with one exception: during the rut. Pre-rut is the best time to spot and stalk big bucks. But if you find yourself in the midst of the rut, you just have to get smarter. The main thing at this time is to watch for those ghostly does. The more does, the more eyes watching your every move. The eyes are the antelopes' best defense. Antelope don't need to be laying next to each other to keep an eye out for one another. More times than not, does will sit off about 200 yards or so, keeping an eye on the buck's back as it sits off to gather some sun. But you can beat the ghostly eyes if you're cautious and patient.

Be patient: Move slowly, keep your eyes up, and watch for does. Better yet, find barriers to walk behind to conceal yourself from all antelope, bucks or does. Move very slowly, and if one happens to look at you, freeze and wait out the situation. If you move, and the animal detects you, you might as well pack it up and head for home. My big buck got up from its bed three times while I was putting

on my stalk. Each time it looked right at me. I held motionless in the crouched position for so long, my legs started to shake from muscle tiredness. But each time the buck got up, I never so much as let out a deep breath. If a buck suspects any danger, he'll disappear faster than any $100 bill on a blackjack table.

Countless hours of trial and error have provided me with extensive knowledge of antelope and how to hunt them, and as a result I have harvested antelope in five consecutive years. Patience and persistence, coupled with total commitment, have led to my success. A hunter should always be ethical and knowledgeable of his game so that he may experience grace along with self-satisfaction. Bowhunting lets me grasp that once-in-a-lifetime feeling even when I'm not successful, but tagging those trophies always caps off all the hard work and effort that goes into being just a plain old hunter.

Ty Robinson
Broadus, MT

quick tip

Hunt Grouse in a Big Wind

Many ruffed grouse hunters stay home when big winds kick up, figuring the grouse will be too spooky or hard to find. Hunters with dogs worry about how the birds' scent will disperse quickly. But a big wind will draw me *to* the grouse coverts, because it will concentrate the birds and make them *easier* to find.

Simply enough, head for the lowest-lying areas; in the flat forests of the Upper Midwest, that means tag alder and other swamps, even if they have some grassy cover. In hilly areas such as in the East and some Midwestern areas, hunt the protected sides and bottoms of draws and gullies. In the Mountain West, head for the canyon bottoms.

Tom Carpenter
Plymouth, MN

Hunt by the Clock

Our group of whitetail fanatics has developed a technique we call "hunting by the clock." We have access to a one-square-mile section of roadless hillside in a rough and brushy area of Washington state. It's a perfect location for whitetails, with brushy clearcuts on two sides and steep, rugged terrain above and below.

We have built four parallel trails across this mile of whitetail paradise. Our "trails" are made by leaning long sticks against trees or piling several stones into a cairn; we put these markers close enough together that we can see from one to the next. Since our trails are natural, they leave no scars on the environment; they're also invisible to any other hunters who don't know our technique. The trails follow terrain and openings, and are about 300 yards apart on average.

On each trail, we've identified stopping places—forked trees, large rocks, etc. These stops are approximately 200 yards apart, and are noted on a map we copy for each hunter. All stops are in open areas, thus ensuring good shooting.

We all start on the trails "by the clock" at the same time. Starting time has been agreed to in advance, and marked on our maps. Each hunter progresses to the first stop identified on his map, and waits at that spot until the specified "move time" (also marked on the maps), when he proceeds to the next stop by still-hunting. Since the trails are well-marked, no one gets lost, which would destroy the timing.

This procedure goes on for the entire mile. All hunters know exactly where the others are at each stop. We often see deer sneaking away from the hunter above or below, and most of us have taken a buck that was quietly slipping away in this fashion.

One of our stops is at a steep, brushy draw. If we have a fourth hunter, he goes on the upper trail and at a specified time comes down the draw, knowing the other hunters will be at specific spots that were chosen to provide a good shooting lane. Once the fourth hunter is done walking through the draw, he proceeds with the lowest hunter for the rest of the session.

Generally, the times between stops allow for very slow movement. We usually use an entire morning for the mile, but this can be adjusted simply by changing the move times.

This procedure can be done anywhere with a few days of scouting and "trail building." You can make as many trails as you need, and since nothing is permanently marked, the trails can be changed and rerouted as experience dictates. Remember to mark all maps with the same starting and move times, and be sure all your watches are synchronized.

Frank Lehrman
Chewelah, WA

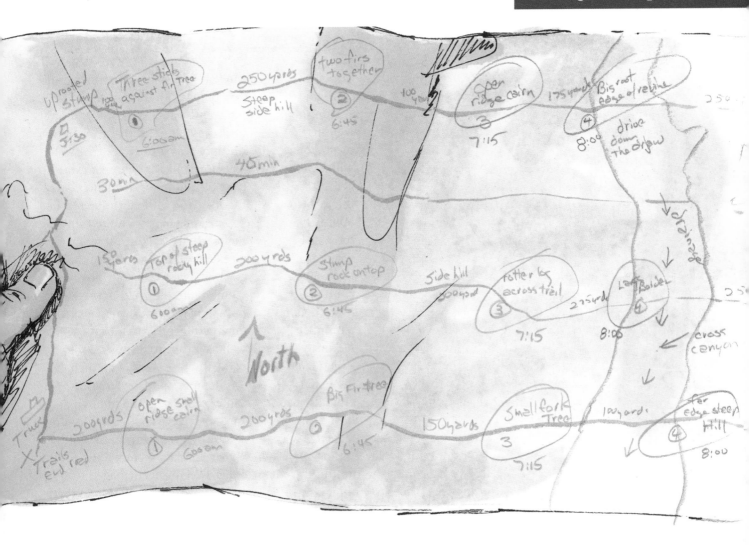

Pig Hunting Tips

Try to avoid shooting pigs in their bedding area if at all possible. This will only serve to disrupt their normal patterns of daily movement and where they will bed. If you take a pig in a feeding or watering area, usually the other pigs will continue their normal daily pattern of movement, as will pigs taken on trails between these locations.

Douglas M. Rodd
Upland, CA

How to Hunt Trophy Big Game ... On Your Own

Like many individuals, my hunting has been limited to self-guided ventures on public land. Hunting on your own, however, doesn't mean you will never get into the record book. Over the last 15 years, I've had the good fortune to take a number of North American big game animals that have qualified for the Boone and Crockett Club.

I think the key to finding trophy big game is to hunt in out-of-the-way places, or under conditions most hunters wouldn't even dream of. Although many of the "experts" might disagree, I am a firm believer that trophy-class animals can be taken on public land by unguided hunters, provided one concentrates on hunting certain areas.

On a larger scale, remote geographical locations are always a good bet. Most big game animals require the security and solitude offered by places that are as far away from development as possible. For me, that means hunting places where there are no roads or trails, or in areas that restrict the use of motorized vehicles. Last spring, I researched an area in southeast Alaska in preparation for a black bear hunt. After talking to the fish and game department, air taxi pilots and other hunters, I pinpointed an area that could only be accessed by floatplane. Although the spot was located in a saltwater bay, it was just far enough away from a number of towns to make it a little too difficult to be reached by smaller boats with their limited fuel capacity. The result was a week-long hunt in an area that's as isolated as you can get. The bears seemed like they had never seen a human before, and we managed to take two record-book bears, as well as a third that missed the books by just 1/16th of an inch.

Remote and isolated areas can also be found on a much smaller scale. What I look for are certain types of terrain that only bigger animals seem willing to tolerate. I've always managed to spot such animals in areas where there is a sudden change in the terrain or landscape.

One example is where the woods or thick growth meets an open area or cultivated field. Another would be a place with fairly flat terrain that borders a lot of rolling hills or small canyons. I remember once when I was hunting in New Mexico I found an area that the locals called "the badlands." This area was completely surrounded by a road on one side, a very steep canyon on the other and some fenced-in rangeland on the remaining two sides. After making a climb from the roadside through some very thick brush, I spooked up not one, but two huge Coues' deer (which I am sorry to say probably died of old age).

Another hangout for trophy-sized big game is "islands." What I am referring to here is a fairly small area that provides food and cover and is surrounded by an open area, or other access points that confine animals to the security of the island.

About 10 years ago I was hunting moose in an area that was very popular with a lot of other hunters. Despite the pressure, there still seemed to be a lot of sign indicating some very big bulls. The other hunters, however, all chose to hunt pretty much the same areas. I noticed that no one wanted to take the time to find a way across a stream that was about six feet deep and about 12 feet wide, especially since after that they would have to hike another 600 yards through muskeg. So my partner and I built a makeshift bridge from spruce trees, and hiked to a wooded area that was a mile long by a half-mile wide. Once there, I called the biggest moose I have ever seen. Unfortunately, my arrow did not find its mark and the big bull left with his estimated 65-inch rack intact. I have also hunted islands made up of alders or willows and have caught animals leaving the area just before dark. Several

The decision to put some distance between ourselves and the guided hunters made all the difference in the world.

years ago I took my best Sitka black-tailed deer after staking out such an area.

Trophy-sized game can also be found in what I call the "middle spots." These are places between high-traffic areas, or somewhere halfway between a highway and the area where the hunting camps are set up.

I was in Montana one year, hunting sheep, and jumped a huge 6-point elk that was hiding out in some thick cover situated between the highway and some hunting camps. I was truly amazed that such a trophy animal could be found in an area that was determined by the local hunters to be too close to the road and not far enough into the mountains. The good moose area that I have referred to above is in a similar location and is situated between two highly traveled rivers.

To find the types of areas I've described, I start by looking at topographical maps or aerial photos. Because my goal is to hunt as many big game species as possible, I am usually hunting an area I've never hunted before. Thus, the only practical way to initially locate the more remote or isolated spots is to study a map or photo in the comfort of my den. For me, finding these "secret" places is a real challenge and in many ways almost as exciting as the hunt itself.

I also find it quite valuable to talk with pilots, road maintenance workers, firefighters, biologists and other people who spend a great deal of time in the outdoors. These individuals can give you a lot of information about habitat, game sightings and access points which will help narrow your search for a particular hot spot. Also, I would not be too quick to dismiss talking with other hunters and even

Continued ...

guides about hunting in a certain area. Frequently, there are places that present too much of a challenge for other hunters. I've talked with many hunters who have described a certain canyon, drainage, swamp or other area as a place where they have seen trophy animals, but they consider that spot "impossible" to hunt. More often than not, what they are talking about is nothing more than having to put out a little more physical effort or forego a nicer camp in order to hunt the area.

A number of years back, I took a record-book Alaska brown bear when my hunting partner and I hiked farther away from the dropoff point than a well-known guide and his two very overweight clients. Although our spike camp consisted of nothing more than a very small tent and a week's worth of freeze-dried food, we were right in the middle of a large drainage that was home to monster brown bears. While I admit that the hike back to base camp with heavy hides was not the highlight of the hunt, the decision to put some distance between ourselves and the guided hunters made all the difference in the world.

I have also had success in finding quality big game right after a storm, or by hunting during a late or extended season. Once when I was hunting caribou, I noticed that right after a squall the larger bulls would leave the main herd and travel along the ridgetops of some nearby hills. With the onset of another storm, I positioned myself within shooting distance of the ridgetops. Almost immediately after the wind and rain stopped, a small group of large bulls appeared, allowing me to take a trophy caribou. On other hunts, deer and bears have

seemed to appear magically right after a hard rain or windstorm. If you can put up with the weather and be at the appointed spot when it breaks, you stand a really good chance of seeing a trophy animal.

You also have a better opportunity to see trophy-sized big game if you can hunt during a late season. Although you will most likely encounter a lot of bad weather and have fewer hunting days, there will also be less competition. You'll also find that the animals are easier to reach and more mobile in the race to prepare for the onset of winter.

One of my very first hunts in Alaska was for Rocky Mountain goats, and took place during a registration hunt in October. Because of the typically bad weather during that time of year, there were no other hunters in one particular drainage that was home to a number of nice goats. Snow had pushed them farther down the mountain and the few days of good weather that we did have allowed us to get close enough to shoot two superb billies. While it is true that late-season hunts can be a real gamble, in many cases this may be all the edge you need.

Hunting the out-of-the-way places or during conditions less favorable to other hunters will give you an opportunity and advantage that I feel puts you on par with guided hunters, or those who can afford to hunt on private land. If you can find these places or are able to schedule your hunt at the end of the season, I know you will have your chance to take that trophy of a lifetime.

Andy Fierro
Chugiak, AK

Make Your Land Deer-Friendly

One of the most important things you can do to improve your whitetail hunting is to make your hunting land deer-friendly. Here are a few of my suggestions.

- Feed your herd year-round.
- Make trails through the thick brush; these help the deer get through it as well as give you an easy path.
- If there is no water source on your hunting ground, do what it takes to make one.
- Plant grasses that deer like to graze on.
- If drought is common where you live, you might want to put in a small irrigation system to help deer foods flourish.

Neil Freytag
Flatonia, TX

FROM THE EXPERT'S NOTEBOOK

Record-Book Tips ... by Jim Shockey

The Importance of Listening

Listen carefully to what the outfitter you intend to book with is telling you. Many hunters crash and burn in a sea of despair because they didn't "listen" when the outfitter told them what the hunt would be like, and hence, came to camp with false expectations. Most hunters are optimists; when the outfitter says that six out of thirty hunters kill record-book animals, most hunters think "Wow! That's great odds." They assume that they'll get one of those animals, and when the hunt is halfway over and they haven't seen what they're looking for, they're disappointed. Yet they shouldn't be; the outfitter told them the facts, but they didn't figure out that their odds of killing one of those record-book animals was only 20%. Put another way, they should have planned to hunt with the outfitter for five years before they could expect to take one of those record-book animals. Heck, they might even go ten times or more without taking one!

Don't Pass Up a Trophy on Opening Day

I've seen many hunters fail to harvest a record-book example of whatever species of animal they are hunting because they saw that animal on the first day of the hunt. This happens even though prior to the hunt, they would have been ecstatic with such an animal! Their reasoning is always the same: because they saw the animal right away, they assume every day of the hunt is going to be as productive. Big mistake! Hunting is never predictable. That's why it's hunting, not shopping. When you go into a hunt, go into it, from the very first minute, prepared to shoot if you see an animal that satisfies your goal. That way you won't spend the entire second half of your hunt searching for the same animal you could have taken on the first day.

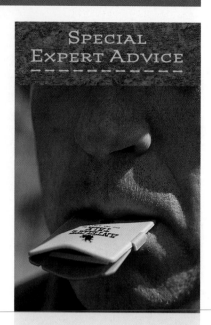

When All the Hunters Leave—Don't

The opening morning of elk season found me in the predawn darkness on a ridge where I could see the opposite slope across the draw below me. A couple days earlier while scouting, I had spotted a bull and several cows in this area, and was now awaiting shooting time with anticipation.

As darkness turned to light, I could see blaze orange swarm over the draw and the hillside across from me. Looking down into the draw, I saw four parked vehicles. Hunters were everywhere. By 9:00 a.m., they had tramped through all the cover and were headed back to their vehicles. During this whole time, I never heard a shot.

After waiting for a while, I walked back to my rig. I drove to the top of the ridge above me and looked around. Although I could see for miles from the ridge, there wasn't a vehicle or hunter in sight. They had all gone somewhere else.

I knew there was a large patch of cover about two miles to the south and over another high ridge. Some of the hunters had gone that way. I looked over the cover below me and figured that if any elk escaped the hunters in that southern area, they would come over the ridge and head to the cover I was looking down on.

There were two draws that the elk would probably come up. The draws met on a saddle about three-fourths of the way to the top. I positioned myself with a good view of both draws. I was confident that I would detect any elk that might be making its way up either draw.

I didn't have long to wait. About ten minutes after I had settled in, a lone bull came up the draw on the east side. When the bull was about 200 yards away, I had a good shot and took it. The elk then disappeared behind a tree, but never came out the other side. I walked over and found the elk dead behind the tree. During the next five hours while I was packing the meat out, I never saw any other elk, never heard a shot, and saw no other hunters.

The moral of this story is: If everyone leaves, it might just pay to hang around and see what they might push your way from where they went.

Jerry Rustad
Kemmerer, WY

quick tip

Calling Antelope

When stalking an antelope, I carry an antelope "bleat" call in my mouth, ready to talk to the animals if I slip up a little and make them nervous. The call will often calm them, and sometimes even draw them toward me. Call sparingly, but loudly enough to be heard over the distance and through the prairie wind. Truth be told, you could even do this with a deer bleat call, if you can't locate an antelope bleat, because in a large part you're just taking advantage of the antelope's innate curiosity.

Tom Carpenter
Plymouth, MN

Figuring Out High-Pressure Patterns

All experienced hunters know that preseason scouting is essential for a successful deer season. The problem is that a couple days of heavy hunting pressure, like that of firearms season, changes everything! The good news is that whitetail deer develop high-pressure patterns. You can learn them by watching other hunters in the tracts of land around your hunting area.

Watching groups of hunters conduct a drive is very useful in learning these patterns. So if you've filled your tag, or the action at your stand is slim-to-nonexistent, get in that truck and take a drive around your hunting area to see what's up!

If you come upon a group conducting a drive, get to a place where you can see as much of the property as possible; you can probably park along the road. The group may be using a CB radio as its primary source of communication (legal in some areas but not in others) and if you have one, you may be able to tune in on the group's channel. Groups that conduct drives often harvest mature bucks that are moving in the area … and wouldn't you like to pattern one of them?

When you watch a drive, it doesn't take long to figure out the escape patterns that the deer are using. Then you can make adjustments in your own hunting area and methods.

David Bartch
Stockton, IL

Stay in Good Shape to Pursue Whitewater Grizzly

I stood beside the gravel strip and watched the twin engine Beechcraft gun its engines and take off north in a cloud of dust toward the town of Telegraph Creek. The Central Mountain Airways plane had departed from Smithers, British Columbia, at 11:00 a.m., landed at a mining camp strip, then unloaded me, my duffel bag and rifle at this strip. I had left Columbia, Maryland at 7:00 a.m. the previous day and overnighted in Smithers, British Columbia. The trip had been normal so far, but I was getting a little concerned because the only sign of civilization was the rough gravel strip beside the Sabine River, a rougher gravel road and a sign that stated that Telegraph Creek was two kilometers north.

A cloud of dust from the north brought a battered Chevy pickup to the strip and out jumped Fred Day. Fred is the eldest son of Fletcher Day, the owner of Tahltan Outfitters. After shaking hands, Fred remarked that he had been expecting a somewhat younger hunter. He explained that we would spend a few days at their base camp on the Chesley River hunting black bears, fishing for steelhead, and maybe get a line on a grizzly, and if that wasn't successful he had obtained a sturdy whitewater rubber raft, which we would use to float the Chesley for 45 miles. I told him I'm sixty-one but am in good physical condition and had hunted in Alaska, British Columbia, Colorado and Montana during the past five years with no problems. He agreed that my condition appeared a lot better than some younger hunters he had guided.

Ron Eastman's Cessna dropped Fred, myself and all our gear at the base camp. As soon as I met my guide Charley Quash, we and Johnny Morrow, another guide, beat it to the river to check for bear sign. We spent the rest of the day scouting and fishing, and Johnny caught a beautiful 12-pound steelhead. We all caught our share of rainbow trout. Charley and I took a long hike upriver the next day, stopping to glass for bears at open areas.

Seniors can enjoy good hunting if they stay in good physical condition. This is important for all hunters who want to hunt where the action is.

It was the second of May. Mark Peterson, Fletcher Day's son-in-law who, handling the booking for Tahltan, had told me in February that this was the best time to hunt grizzly bears as they would be out of hibernation and roaming the rivers and mountainsides fishing and looking for winter kills. Tahltan's area consists of 3,000 square miles of mountains and 65 miles of the Chesley River from their base camp to the Nylan River, where they have a fishing and goat camp that was our final destination.

Although this was the fourth grizzly tag I'd gotten in British Columbia, I had never taken one. I had been in a spring hunt out of Prince George's and gotten a nice black bear, and also had two fall hunts out of Prince George's and Fort St. Johns, so I was really anxious to get a nice grizzly. Mark felt my chances were about 80 percent as I would be starting my 14-day hunt on the opening day.

After hunting the first day with me, Charley told Fred I could keep up with him so we were ready to go. The next four days were spent out of a spike camp downriver. On the seventh day, we spotted a nice black bear that was feeding on kenticuk berries near the top of a slide. We hiked up the mountain to shorten the range, but the bear heard or scented us and started moving higher. The range was between 250 and 300 yards, and my .338 Win. Mag. with 250-grain Federal Nosler Partitions made the task fairly easy. We had scoped more than thirty black bears in those seven days, and the one I took was the biggest we had seen.

The next morning Fred, Charley and I loaded our gear, food and guns into the Zodiak raft; with me in the front, the gear in the middle and Fred and Charley in the rear to steer, we started down the river. We'd had a lot of rain on the fifth and sixth days; plus, the snow in the high country was melting due to warmer weather. As a result, the river was rising and was quite swift, which prevented fishing for trout for breakfast and supper.

This was the first time the Days had floated the Chesley River. They had used a 16-foot jon boat equipped with a 75hp jet to run up the river to hunt bears and moose, but no one had hunted the river below. We were all excited to be on this trip—me because I always hunt like the next ten seconds could be the best of my life, and them because this was their native land and they would see it all for the first time. Fred's grandfather, a former chief of the Tahltan Indian tribe, had been down this river and warned Fred of some bad water, particularly a canyon we could have trouble in.

The first day of the float trip was fairly calm and was spent observing geese, ducks, beavers, moose and an occasional black bear, one of which swam across the river right in front of us. On the second day, we spotted a large black bear on a bluff and beached the raft to take a better look. When we got out, Fred found fresh tracks of a large grizzly paralleling the river, which charged us all up.

Charley, as good guides do, was glassing a canyon in back of us and spotted a grizzly feeding high on the side. Fred wanted to continue downriver in the direction of the fresh tracks. Charley asked me what I wanted to do. The grizzly was so far away that he couldn't be sure of the size. I elected to check the grizzly out.

We changed the hip boots for leather boots, shed our coats and started up the side of the canyon. After two hours of climbing, we were in snow up to our knees, but it was quite warm and the mosquitoes were having a field day. We finally got to an outcropping where we could see, and found that the grizzly had moved on.

We ate a late lunch from our packs and enjoyed the view. We could see Nylan Mountain way to the south and the stretch of river we would float down. I was overwhelmed by the wild and powerful scene of the towering snow-capped mountains, vast forest and the twisting swift river, and the fact that I was involved in an adventure no modern-day hunter had undertaken on the river.

We made our way down through the melting snow to the floor of the canyon, hoping to pick up the grizzly's tracks, but didn't find any. We got back to our raft by 5 p.m. and headed down the river, which was getting higher and rougher. We had gone probably two miles and were in some fairly deep and quiet water. The river made a curve to the right and as it did, Charley quickly whispered, "Grizzly, right side."

The bear was walking downriver, about a hundred yards away from us. I quietly worked the bolt on the .338 Win. Mag. while they backed up and steadied the bouncing raft. I aimed at the bear's left shoulder and squeezed off a round. The bear went down, sat up and let out a tremendous roar. I hit the bear again, spinning it around on the gravel bar, then fired a third time. The bear had been rolling and growling but on

Continued …

the third shot, it collapsed into the river. Fred and Charley started paddling frantically. The bear was floating faster than we were and Fred remarked that his uncle had a grizzly sink in a similar situation, so we were quite concerned. We finally were able to get in front of the bear. Charley poked the grizzly with a paddle to be sure it was dead.

I got a rope on its paw and we floated the bear to the bank. We all were delirious—me from finally getting my grizzly, and Charley and Fred from having guided a successful hunt. After taking photos, we skinned out the bear. I was amazed at the animal's size. It was an old bear. Its front teeth were worn down, one fang was broken, his right ear had a healed split. There was a scar on its hip from an earlier battle. The golden-brown fur was in its prime with no rubs.

We set up the two-way radio and reported our success to base camp. We told them we planned to continue downriver for two days, and made arrangements for Ron to fly us out at that time. That night I could hardly sleep from the excitement of the hunt, and also the knowledge that the sandbar we were camped on was in prime grizzly country. Our rifles next to our sleeping bags offered some company.

The next morning, we were into rough water, and now had an additional hundred pounds of green bear skin in our little raft. The river changed to sharp turns, extreme inclines and narrow channels. We shot through the sluices at great speed and connected with hidden boulders on a regular basis. Charley and Fred worked constantly to keep the raft straight in the river's vicious current. Not being sure where the really bad water was and remembering the warning from Fred's grandfather, we stopped and walked ahead to check whenever there was a right turn in the river. Charley and Fred worked the

raft through several rapids while I walked the bank with the rifle, alert for bears. We did encounter a big grizzly on one of these checks. It was on the opposite bank coming toward us. Suddenly the bear caught our scent, looked up and with two jumps disappeared into the bush. It just as easily could have crossed the river in the same two jumps. Fred and Charley had both been chased and treed by grizzlies and have the greatest respect for them, as do all people who guide and work in their range.

We arrived at the canyon in the river in the afternoon. The water was so high and the sides so sheer that we had no choice but to ride it out. We went through at great speed. Charley, attempting to avoid a large boulder, broke his paddle. The raft struck the boulder and tipped to the right. We all leaned to the left and luckily the raft broke loose and shot on through the canyon. The water calmed a little and we observed several goats feeding along the rim; shortly after, three moose watched us float by while they continued feeding. What a thrill to know none of them had ever seen a human. We saw several more grizzlies, black bears and moose the rest of the way to Nylan.

Roger Britton, a taxidermist in Smithers, British Columbia, is working on a full mount of my grizzly. The bear is 8 feet 2 inches, nose to tail. The skull measures 24 inches green. This bear will be my monument to all the great hunts I've had the privilege to take in the magnificent wilderness of British Columbia. My reason for writing this story is to point out that seniors can enjoy good hunting if they stay in good physical condition. This is important for all hunters, regardless of age, who want to hunt where the action is.

Eldon Hart

Continuous Calling for Turkeys

Fall turkey hunting in Wisconsin is pretty much a "right place/right time" proposition. Unlike during spring, birds won't answer your call, and because the birds are grouped together, your odds of fooling a single bird are virtually nonexistent. Hunting from a blind, while effective in the spring, can seem like a waste of time in the fall.

On a recent fall hunt, however, I was able to take a nice gobbler from a blind by trying a slightly unusual tactic.

The first day, I hunted from dawn until sunset, but neither saw nor heard anything. My confidence in the blind location I'd chosen began to drop. However, I had taken a good bird here in the spring, and the setup looked right, so I decided to stick with it.

The next morning, I was in my blind before first light. I heard two hens yelp in different directions, so I knew there were at least two flocks in the area. I answered the hens, but by 9:00 a.m. two small deer and a squirrel were the only excitement provided.

There was a fair amount of wind, so I decided to try "continuous calling." Over the years, I've watched hens come into my decoys and noticed that they were constantly clucking and purring while feeding. I reasoned it was worth a try.

After I had been calling almost continuously for two hours, a fine gobbler calmly strutted into my decoys, literally touching the one jake in my spread. Since I hadn't seen him approach, I was still calling when he came into my spread.

He seemed much less suspicious than any of the 10 or so gobblers I've taken. I'm convinced that the continuous clucking and purring not only brought the tom in, but helped sell the decoy illusion.

If you try this tactic, my advice is to play the wind. You'll need to call more loudly and more often on windy days. But like me, you might be pleasantly surprised.

Robert J. Fehring
Green Lake, WI

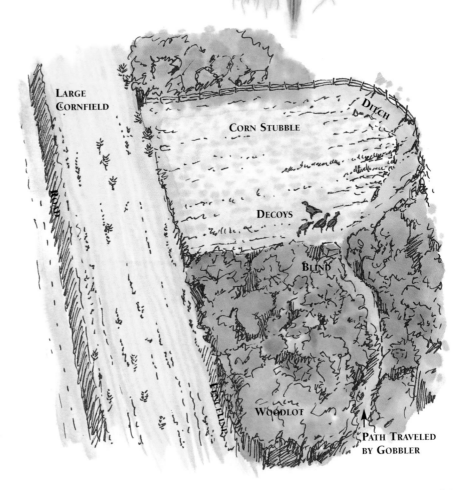

LARGE CORNFIELD

DITCH

CORN STUBBLE

DECOYS

BLIND

WOODLOT

PATH TRAVELED BY GOBBLER

SPECIAL EXPERT ADVICE

quick tip

Top Spot for Cottontails

My A-Number-One, all-time favorite spot for jumping a cottontail is not the venerable old brush pile. Yes, you'll flush a lot of bunnies there, out of the briar patch or cane patch, from the old junkpile in a gully, or around an abandoned homestead. But *always* investigate when you see this particular hiding spot: a downed tree limb that has been there long enough to have tall grass growing around and within the branches. The combination of woody and grassy cover seems to appeal to bunnies as a hiding spot. If the grassy-downed-tree juts into a hayfield, other cropfield or meadow, all the better; good hiding with good food a hop away.

Tom Carpenter
Plymouth, MN

FROM THE EXPERT'S NOTEBOOK

Complete Camouflage ... by Glenn Sapir

Although you may deck yourself out in camouflage clothing from head to toe, you may be overlooking some key points.

For instance, when you are turkey hunting, you will likely set up against a tree. You'll be seated with your knees up in front of you and your shotgun at the ready on your knee.

Are the soles of your boots exposed, and if so, are they light-colored? How about the sleeves of your shirt or jacket—do they ride up and expose bare skin when you position yourself for the shot? The same with your pant legs: do they ride up over your boots, exposing white or red-trimmed socks or bare shins?

Go through a dress rehearsal before the season. You might find you need longer-sleeved shirts, longer-legged pants, different gloves with longer wrist bands or new boots (or, at least, soles that must be colored). You should also replace your socks with high ones that are dark grey, brown or green.

Bare skin and white, red or blue colors may alert a turkey to your presence, and could fool another hunter into making a tragic mistake.

Lessons Learned from Dad

I can remember back to my early years, growing up in a small northern California town called Montague. My dad was a logger all his life. He operated a Caterpillar tractor and built logging and U.S. Forest Service roads.

Dad always got up early and went off to work, except on his days off when he would sleep until 7:00 a.m. But in the fall of the year, he would get up early on his days off and have breakfast; then a friend would come by. I can still recall Dad and his friend talking over a couple cups of coffee. Then Dad would grab a thermos of coffee, a couple egg sandwiches and his trusty "Ol' Betsy" as he called his model 94 Winchester .32 Special. Then Dad and his friend would drive off into the early morning darkness.

Sometimes they didn't get back until after dark, and often they would have one or two nice muley bucks. I could see how excited they were as they took care of their game and talked about the day's adventure. I would get so excited watching them, I couldn't wait until I was old enough to go hunting. When that day finally came, I was very excited; and after all these years, I still get excited! From that day and on into the future, I learned valuable lessons I have passed on to my own children and grandchildren.

That was almost 60 years ago, and Dad is no longer with us. But when I'm out hunting, I can still hear my dad like he is right there whispering in my ear those tips and strategies from yesteryear.

"Son, always remember when going into a new hunting area, try to locate a high peak in the direction you are hunting; also locate a high peak behind you. Hunt the area between these peaks and you will not get lost.

"Son, on an early afternoon hunt down a ridgetop, move slow and easy. Don't forget to stop, look and listen. Sit and glass the draws and the other ridgetops; it's a good way to spot a bedded buck.

"Son, always remember when you spot game to check the background before you shoot. It's better to be safe than sorry.

"Son, when you're getting ready to shoot a buck that's below you in steep country and you're shooting downhill, aim at the buck's front knees and you will hit him low behind the shoulders in a vital area." I have done this a few times, and it really works!

Hunters don't just go out to kill; we enjoy the challenge of a hunt and the time out in the field with family and friends. If we get our deer or elk, it makes the outing more enjoyable and provides meat to feed the family for winter. The strategies and tips and the many memories we have of our dads, other family members and friends are what bring all of us to enjoy the hunt. "Thanks, Dad!"

Charles E. Richardson
Belgrade, MT

This whitetail buck was taken during a hunting trip out of Ashland, Montana, in Custer National Forest. I told my hunting partner we should hunt the ridgetops. He took my advice and bagged this nice buck with one shot. It has a total of 13 points. He allowed me to get my mug in this photo!

Honey Burn for Black Bears

During a fall black bear hunt in northern Ontario, my friend and hunting partner Mike Perkins and I were having a pretty tough time seeing any bears because they were only hitting our baits after dark. After four days of not seeing any bears, Mike suggested we try a trick he had heard of called a honey burn. With nothing to lose I quickly agreed, so we went to the local hardware store and got everything we needed.

When I arrived to my stand area that evening, I prepared my honey burn set-up. I was in my treestand by 4:45 p.m. It was a beautiful fall evening, with the sun shining and a temperature of about 50°F.

The smell of the honey was almost heavenly and it seemed to attract lots of attention because other animals and birds started to appear almost like magic. My visitors included two pine martens, several whiskey jacks and even a few ruffed grouse and spruce grouse.

As the smoke slowly began to diminish, I was beginning to wonder if I was going to get a chance to see a bruin on this gorgeous evening because the sun was already beginning to go behind the trees. Suddenly, though, a beautiful black boar appeared, making a beeline for the bait. I watched this magnificent creature in total awe for about five minutes before harvesting it with one shot from my Remington 700. My first black bear hunt was now a success.

Without the help and guidance of my friend Mike—and some easy-to-find supplies like honey—I may have come home with nothing but the memory of a pleasant evening in my stand. Instead, I also have a beautiful trophy to show for it as well.

Remember this easy method if you're ever in a similar situation, but check your region's game laws first. A honey burn is great when bears have gone nocturnal. The sweet smell of the honey makes them come in when conventional baiting isn't moving them until after dark.

James Bancroft
Lansing, MI

Honey Burn "Recipe"

What you will need:

- Jar of honey
- Large empty soup can (28-oz. can)
- Portable sterno-type stove
- Can of Sterno (2-hour can)

Select an area near your stand that you'll be able to keep an eye on. Clear away all leaves, sticks, grass, etc., to avoid starting a fire. Place the stove in the cleared area. Set the can on the stove and add about two inches of honey. Light the stove. After a few minutes the honey will begin to boil and, eventually, to burn. This will create smoke with a very pungent aroma that will permeate the area.

Note: Don't put too much honey in the can, or it may boil over and extinguish the stove. Two inches is enough for 1½ to 1¾ hours.

Hunting for a Bull

On a cold November morning, I was getting ready to go hunting with my dad, Dennis, and my good friend, Jim. It had snowed two days earlier, so conditions would be brisk. At about 4:00 a.m., we got into two trucks and drove about 30 minutes from our homes into the mountains of Montana.

My dad was going to park up near a gate on a high road and walk toward my truck, which I was going to park lower down after dropping Jim off at a different gate a mile up the road. After dropping Jim off, I went back to a third gated road where I had planned to start that morning. I began walking.

I walked for about an hour, then stopped to wait for full daybreak. As I waited, I heard something coming through the crusty snow. I got excited and scanned the area with my binoculars, but it was only a whitetail doe and fawn. They were walking up a draw, so I walked down the road to the point where it met the draw. We met there at the same time; they spooked and took off.

As I walked down the road some more, I came to a place where a herd of elk had come off the hill and onto the road I was walking. I also found a large bedding area. I felt the tracks and the beds. They were frozen, so I knew they were from the previous evening. I started following the tracks, and soon came to a spot where the road ended abruptly at a ridge. I climbed up the ridge and sat down on a stump. There was another road on the other side of the ridge, and soon I saw three cow elk about 200 yards down this other road.

As soon as the cows turned a corner in the road, I jumped to my feet and hit the road running. I got to the corner and saw a big logging operation around the corner. Elk were milling around above and below the road by this logging operation. I glassed the elk to see if I could pick out any bulls among the many cows. Soon I found a spike and a 3-point bull, and finally I saw a nice 5-point bull.

I put my crosshairs on the bull's chest and squeezed off a shot. The bull flinched and took off running down the hill. I chambered another bullet and fired again, and the bull was down for good. It was a great feeling.

My dad and Jim came by about a half-hour later to help me with preparations to get the bull out. I was proud of my elk, and glad that I had been able to take advantage of the situation to track this herd.

Curtis Deschamps
Colorado Springs, CO

Try Woodcock—Nature's Odd Bird

wings as they twist and turn through the thickets, dodging limbs and trees to make their getaway. With their extremely long bills they resemble a cross between a bat and a giant mosquito. Woodcock use their long bills to probe soft ground for earthworms, their preferred food.

As if all of this isn't enough oddities for one little bird, there is more. The females are larger than the males, and they even migrate at different times. Woodcock smell so strange that some dogs refuse to retrieve them.

In their courtship, the males perform a bizarre aerial dance to attract the females. It has been claimed, though not proven to my knowledge, that woodcock hens will sometimes carry their young between their feet. I did flush a female with young one spring when I was hunting for mushrooms. I didn't see her carry her young, but she kept flying close by as the young walked around with their wings held out, calling for her with those long beaks. It was very comical to watch them.

October means the beginning of woodcock season in the Ohio Valley, even though few hunters go after this little gamebird. There are many reasons for this. Woodcock are strange birds. In fact, nearly everything about them is odd.

Woodcock are nocturnal, feeding just after dark and returning to the thickets and woods to rest during the day. Their eyes are placed high on their heads so they can see even behind for approaching danger. Their ears are beneath their eyes. Soft brown feathers cover their quail-sized body, with dark bands on the head and spots on their plumage that make them blend in perfectly with the forest floor. Since they are camouflaged so well, often they will not flush unless you nearly step on them.

Once flushed, woodcock make an odd whistling sound with their

Woodcock are in the sandpiper family as are snipe, but are upland birds, which makes them different from all other sandpipers. If you know a little about woodcock, you know that they are not very difficult to hunt. Early-season hunting is the most challenging, because the birds are in wet places like the edges of wooded swamps. The thick vegetation also makes for difficult shooting. Rather than hunt during this frustrating time, I like to wait until their migration

Once flushed, woodcock make an odd whistling sound with their wings as they twist and turn through the thickets.

starts before hunting them. If you know where birds were the year before, there's a good chance they will be there again this year. Habitat changes over time, though, and the birds will move to different locations if this happens.

A good way to determine if the woodcock migration is underway is to watch the sky about one-half hour after sunset, when the birds go out to feed. They like to follow watercourses like streams and creeks. They also like to rest in thickets close to streams or adjacent to fields. The migration will vary with the weather, but is usually well underway by mid-November in the Ohio Valley. It usually is over by early December. If you see several birds, especially in pairs, you know that the migration is underway.

After you hunt woodcock for a while, you can feel if a thicket should hold birds or not. A hunter alone can flush and bag woodcock, but a dog makes the job a lot easier. A downed bird in thick cover is nearly impossible to find

without a dog. Labs won't point, but they will flush woodcock and are expert at finding downed birds. Other breeds of bird dogs will point, but as I said earlier some will refuse to pick up a woodcock. I've never had this problem with labs.

Before you head to the thickets for woodcock, you need to know what kind of gun, choke and shot to use. I like a 20 gauge because it is light to carry. A short barrel is almost a necessity in thick cover. And the more open the choke, the better. Improved cylinder is good; cylinder bore is even better.

Most birds will be very close and you need a big pattern to hit them without tearing them apart. I once shot one in half because I shot too soon. I like to use No. 8 shot, although No. 7½ will work well also. You don't need a heavy load; light loads easily bring down woodcock at the typical range of 15 to 30 yards.

If you bag any woodcock, you will have to find a good way to cook them. Some people swear woodcock are the best-tasting birds in the world. (I prefer quail, but each to his own taste.) Woodcock don't taste bad—just different. But what would you expect from a bird that is so odd it has the nickname "timberdoodle"?

Ken Barnes
Bristow, IN

SPECIAL EXPERT ADVICE

quick tip

Talking to Ducks

Calling ducks is similar to calling big game or predators: most folks tend to call too much. Ducks have their own language. Unfortunately, humans don't speak "duck" fluently any more than we could carry on an intelligent conversation with a baboon! So why tell a duck a story? I'm being a smart-aleck here, but my point is this: the less you call, the less chance there is that the ducks will figure out that you are an imposter. Call only enough to get the quarry's attention, and then just enough to convince the birds to come check things out.

Pick a call that is easy to blow. If you are relatively new to duck calling, learn a good hail call, a contented feeding call and a subtle drake call. That's all you need. In addition, get out and slip up on some ducks regularly where you can lay and listen. Take some notes back with you, and practice!

Jim Van Norman
Edgerton, WY

Worth a Thousand Words

It can be difficult to describe the lay of the land in a hunting area to a hunting partner who has never before walked the land. Words are often inadequate. How about creating a three-dimensional model as a visual aid to your explanation? Take a couple of cakes of children's modeling clay to your hunting camp. The clay can be shaped to describe and illustrate the various hills, creeks and ravines of a hunting area.

Charles Horejsi
Missoula, MT

THE EXPERT'S NOTEBOOK

BIG GAME TIPS ...
by Bob Robb

Elk Hunting: Let Other Hunters Do the Work

Just before opening morning of hunting season, is your "secret" spot suddenly invaded by a horde of other hunters? Don't despair—let the other guys work for you, not against you.

Well before first light, climb high and set up in a saddle leading to a thick escape area. Then, when the other hunters begin beating the brush below you, they might just act as drivers, sending the elk through the saddle—and right past your sights.

Bear Hunting: Fool Their Noses

When hunting black bears over bait where legal, try leaving a rag soaked with your favorite insect repellent hanging over your baitpile for several days before you hunt there. That way, bears will associate the smell of your repellent with food, and not be repelled themselves when they smell a bug dope-soaked hunter sitting on stand nearby.

BOB ROBB

Form a Hunting Club

Make your deer hunting more effective, more successful, and especially, more enjoyable by developing a club or network of hunting friends. I was lucky when, after only a couple years of hunting, I had three good buddies who wanted to form a bowhunting club. After much deliberation about the name of the club, a simple choice was made: *The Four Deer Nuts.* After all, we were all "nuts" about deer! In addition to myself, the club consists of my brother and two good friends.

The main reason we started the club was that we all hunted on the same property, and we were bumping into each other before and after hunting. But soon after making our alliance, we found that our success rate drastically increased. We each now had three other hunters to help with scouting, tracking and stand placement. We found ourselves target

practicing together and helping each other with equipment problems when they cropped up. In addition, a little friendly competition has us always trying new hunting techniques and methods that we might not have attempted otherwise. It's good to have hunting friends to talk to when your season is not going as planned. And when I get home from a successful hunt, I have three friends eager to hear my story.

As our club matured, we lost the hunting rights to our original bowhunting property, and we all started families. These two events separated the four of us somewhat, and our club relationship has proved to be invaluable. We now all have different hunting spots, but on any given day or night, we can always find at least one "nut" to help with

tracking or dragging chores. We meet almost every weekend during the hunting season to butcher and process any deer we might have gotten. We pooled our funds together to buy a walk-in cooler, and we all store our deer there. We conduct other activities together after the hunting season is over, like scouting new property, making hunting videos, and having game dinners for hunters and non-hunters alike.

There is a strong bond that has formed between the four of us, and it has now extended to include some of our other hunting friends. Since we began our friendships, our families have grown, and we look forward to the days our children can hunt together with us.

In summary, if you're just getting started hunting, or if you have been hunting alone for a while, take a tip from The Four Deer Nuts. Develop a club or network of hunting friends to make your hunting season more enjoyable and effective. Share the outdoor experience with friends and family, enjoy the pleasures of nature, and become more successful as a hunter.

William Trout Jr.
Bridgeton, NJ

ABOVE: *The Four Deer Nuts (est. 1986). Left to right: Will Trout, Kyle Trout, Tim Swift and Dave Hemple.*

Persistence Pays Off

It was deer season in Missouri. I had hunted hard from Saturday (the first day of the season) through Tuesday, with nothing to show for it. I had seen some deer but nothing that I really wanted. I had to work Wednesday and Thursday, but got back to the woods to hunt Friday morning. Friday turned out to be one of those days that would test the most devoted hunter.

I woke up Friday morning to get out in the woods early. It was raining steadily, but I got dressed, headed out and crossed an ankle-deep creek along the way.

It was pouring and the wind was so bad for much of the day that it rained sideways. I walked most of the day because I figured the deer wouldn't be up and around; nothing in its right mind would be out in this weather.

I hadn't seen anything all day. Soaked to the bone and chilled, I finally gave up around 3:00 p.m. I started back to the truck, but by this time the little creek was over knee deep and rolling fast! It took me a while to cross the creek. I finally crawled over a fallen tree that was lying across the creek. (I wouldn't recommend that anyone ever try this route … one missed step and you're in the water headed downstream. Fortunately, I made it across without any mishaps, thinking all the while that I used to be more coordinated.)

Soaked and cold, I was just glad to make it back to the truck. I headed home, got out of my wet clothes and crawled into bed to try to warm up. It was more than an hour before I felt warm again.

After going through all that, I had almost given up on hunting Saturday. But earlier in the week my nephew had told me he'd seen several does in the field every morning he hunted. I had an any-deer permit, and taking a doe looked very good to me at this point.

I didn't really feel like crossing the creek again, so I called my nephew and asked a little more about where he had been hunting. He had filled his tag earlier in the week by shooting a nice 6-point buck and said he would be glad to take me out and show me the spot in the morning.

I had gotten my nephew started hunting by taking him out years before. He is in his 30s now, so having him take me out sounded like fun. I think he felt it was his chance to show how good a hunter he had become, even though he couldn't take his gun this time because he had tagged out.

In the morning, I picked him up. We stopped and talked to the landowner so he would know where we were going and what my truck looked like. We were off,

Be Prepared for Action

I own a ranch in Gilroy, California, by the Coyote Reservoir. At one time I lived there, but for the last five years I've been living in Santa Clara with my wife and two boys.

Wild boars are my favorite quarry to hunt, followed by black bears and wild turkeys. There are plenty of hogs on the ranch, as well as turkeys and an abundance of other game. I often take people on pig hunts. I've taken plenty of trophy hogs and plenty of meat hogs. Depending on weather and time of year, I employ different hunting methods.

Most of the time, I spot-and-stalk. During hot, dry weather I can catch the pigs at watering holes and wallows. After a good mud bath, they head down for a nice tree to rub on. The rub marks are clearly visible on the trees. When it's really dry and hot, I can crawl up in the brush and get one out of a bedding area.

To locate pigs, scout your area and know your surroundings. Look for fresh sign. Learn the routes the animals take to get to water, and know where their feeding areas are. Acorn is a favorite food, so if you can find an acorn area you have a good spot to look for pigs.

Pigs like to bed down on brushy hillsides near water. The old trophy boars usually travel alone. If there are barbed-wire fences, check the bottom strands because pigs always leave a few hairs going under the wire. Look for rubs on trees; once you find them, you can pretty well guess that the pigs will be back.

Evening hunts are usually best from a good stand near feeding or rooting areas. Other times, I hunt in the morning. I like to get to a good spot well before first light and wait for the pigs to head back to their bedding areas.

One evening, I was out on a pig hunt. It was getting close to dark when a nice pig presented me with a broadside shot. I squeezed off and got a hit. The pig went in a half-circle, and then ran to the other side of a knoll. I waited about ten minutes and started walking in that direction. By this time, it was getting darker by the minute. I got to the knoll but couldn't spot anything. I walked about 20 yards farther, and suddenly was right on top of the injured pig. It jumped up and hooked me in the leg. As I fell over backwards, I fired a round into the air. The pig ran into the thick brush, so I went and got my flashlight and my .357 revolver.

When I got to the spot, I could see blood all over. I followed the trail on hands and knees, going 25 yards into the brush, before I came upon the dead pig. The lesson here is that you should always have a good flashlight on evening hunts.

I also killed a nice black bear by hunting with hounds on opening day last season. My advice on this method is to be in really good shape. On this particular hunt, I was with

Mike Smith, who is a friend and guide. We got into a 3½-hour chase with the dogs. After the bear was treed we had to hike a mile downhill to get to the bear, then had to hike that same mile back uphill with full packs. This is very rigorous hunting, and if you're not in good shape you won't be able to keep up.

My final advice is to use caution, especially when hunting dangerous animals like pigs and bears. Never underestimate a wounded animal. I've been charged by hogs and have shot them at very close range. I was lucky when I came upon that pig in the brush, because I wasn't hurt badly and the worst harm he did was to ruin a good pair of hunting boots.

Michael Allen
Santa Clara, CA

Missed Opportunities & Second Chances

Almost anyone who has been hunting whitetail for any length of time can tell you stories about missed opportunities. It may be a shot gone wrong, a shot not taken, or an "I-don't-understand-how-I-missed-that" shot. Whichever, it equals a missed opportunity, not a successful harvest.

It was the second day of rifle season, on a five-day hunting trip in Madison County, Arkansas. We had 14 hunters in camp, four of whom were boys.

My 12-year-old son, Josh, and I had "our spot." A "spot" is your choice of woods off-limits to your hunting buddies, unless you grant them permission to hunt there. "Spots" are generally where you have harvested deer or have had opportunities.

When Josh was ten, he harvested a doe at 67 yards through the woods with his .30-30 Win. rifle. That day will always be my most exciting hunt, even though I lost a really nice buck that I was sure I had hit, which we didn't find in two days of tracking.

This year Josh set up a ground blind on the other side of a pond not too far from our regular ground blind. On our first day of hunting, Josh missed a doe. (The night before he had bragged how he would never miss. Now he knows the taste of missed opportunity and he got his shirt tail cut.) I didn't have a shot all day.

Second day, on the morning hunt, I saw a fork-horn buck. This isn't a legal buck in Arkansas, which for the second year has a "three-point rule" (three points or more on one side).

Around 10:30 a.m. Josh came to my blind. He had seen two forkhorns and what he thought to be a 10-pointer that wouldn't come out of the brush. Wow! The deer were on the move. But our stomachs convinced us to go to camp. When we reached camp, my brothers, Perry and Todd, had just finished hanging a nice 6-pointer that Todd had shot.

We ate lunch and everyone shared what they had experienced that morning. Then we headed back to hunt. I spotted movement from the same direction the forkhorn had come that morning. It was a deer moving across through the woods. I didn't need the binoculars to tell that it was a legal deer; in fact, it looked like about an 8-pointer. I thought again of the one I had missed a few years earlier.

As the buck walked from right to left, I made a few rapid grunts on my call. The buck stopped but was behind so many trees I couldn't see well. When it started to walk again, it was going away from me. I hit the grunt again. No response. I raised my rifle with safety off and aimed out in front of where the buck was walking. The buck stepped in front of my sights, and I fired. It jumped and kicked out with its back legs. It ran in the direction it had been walking, then cut back to the right and disappeared up the ridge.

Wow! What a nice buck. I hurdled the blind immediately and ran to where I thought the buck was walking. Oh no! I went back and forth and saw no blood. I thought I would pass out with shock if I had missed this buck.

Josh came over and I told him I thought I had hit a nice 8-pointer. I got back in the blind and pointed Josh in the direction the deer had been walking. "Right there, mark that spot!" I yelled.

Before, I hadn't gone far enough. I went to where Josh was and we started looking. About 10 yards farther, Josh found lung blood all over the ground.

Then we were really excited, because we knew it was a kill shot. We followed the trail, almost running, for 70 or 80 yards, then nothing. The blood trail had stopped. I had Josh stand at the last place we had seen the blood. I made a circle—nothing. Then I made a larger circle, and suddenly hollered "There it is!"

I had harvested my best buck ever. (Well, only my fifth buck ever.) When Josh spotted the antlers standing so far off the ground, "excited" does not begin to describe how he felt. We counted 16 points on that big buck, including 12 points that were more than 1 inch long.

A successful harvest is bringing home a deer. A successful hunt is every time you go, whether you fire a shot or not.

I ran back to my blind to get my camera. On the way, I stepped off how far the shot was. I hadn't realized it was 98 yards. I shoot open sights with an old military gun my dad has had for more than 40 years. I normally practice at 50 yards. Man, I couldn't believe that big buck was mine.

We looked the deer over. I had hit him about 6 inches back and high. But it did the job. We took a few pictures, then field dressed the deer. I sent Josh to get the four-wheeler and to find my brother, Todd; we knew he would be in "his spot."

Forty-five minutes later, Todd showed up and was very excited for me. As we dragged the deer, I told him: "I know you won't believe me, but the one two years ago had a bigger rack."

I had made the shot at about 1:00 p.m. A couple hours later we had the deer hanging in camp. A few more pictures … counting points … checking over the deer. What's this? I find a bump under the hide in the neck. Then I find a healed hole on the other side of the neck. It *is* the buck from two years ago!

The next morning, I headed to Jack's Pawn in Fayetteville to check in the buck. Josh didn't want to go town with me on Monday, so I had my friend, George, hunt our spot with Josh. George sat in my ground blind, "my spot," and shot a 7-pointer and a doe. He had them both checked in by noon.

Two years earlier, I had a *missed opportunity*. I had dropped a buck with a large rack a few yards from my ground blind. The shot was in the neck. I have heard the pros say "When they're down don't push 'em." So I waited. The buck had gone down slinging its head on the ground and kicking in a circle. I was having a victory party of excitement when the buck suddenly jumped up and ran down the mountain. I had waited 10 minutes, only to watch him disappear into the dense evening fog.

A *second chance* at a monster buck proved to be the same as my first chance. When my dad and I skinned the deer, we got the lead from the bullet. When he was cutting up the meat he also found the copper casing that goes over the lead. There's no guarantee that it's the same deer, but I believe it is.

The word *luck* gets used a lot when hunting, and I say it too. But I count it a blessing to even have the opportunity to see a deer in the wild. To harvest one is even a greater blessing.

A *successful harvest* is bringing home a deer. A *successful hunt* is every time you go, whether you fire a shot or not. My philosophy is to enjoy nature and to share experiences with my hunting buddies. I also cherish the time I spend with my hunting partner, my son.

Jeff Mott
Omaha, AR

quick tip

Windy-Day Turkeys

If you wake up in the morning to a howling wind during turkey season, don't roll over and go back to sleep. Head out to an open field, large or small. When the wind is howling, turkeys like to get out in the open because the wind compromises their hearing. I missed my first opportunity at a turkey with my bow for that very reason. I went back to sleep instead of heading out, and when I went to my hunting area later in the morning there were two toms ten yards in front of my blind. Lesson learned!

Randy Lambert
Simcoe, ONT

THE EXPERT'S NOTEBOOK

Take a Stand for Turkeys ... by Mark Kayser

By the middle of the turkey season, it seems like most of the gobblers have become call-shy and won't react or respond to a call. When the gobblers in my area take that attitude, I begin patterning them like a whitetail and intercept them on their daily routine. Once I've patterned the birds, I either build a blind or hide in a deadfall and wait for the birds to wander by my location. I usually place a couple of decoys nearby and use subtle calls when they arrive.

MARK KAYSER

A One-Man Drive for Whitetails

Like many hunters, I own hunting property, and mine has a nice cabin. My place is located in New York State and we mainly hunt the wonderful whitetail. The camp may be full with six or eight of my fellow hunters; we may hunt in pairs, or sometimes alone. Being the host, I let the others make their choice of hunting areas each day. Then I usually hunt alone in one of the other areas.

How do you make a one-man deer drive through the front door of heavy cover while still covering the back door?

Some of the areas I go to are covered with very thick brush or mountain laurel, while others are in nearly impenetrable swamps. There's no way to get into or through such areas without alerting "ye old big buck" and giving him a chance to slip out the back door.

So the challenge I face is how to make a one-man drive in the front door while still covering the back door. I don't remember how I came up with the solution, but I can tell you that it works. Here's my technique.

Oh, I almost forgot a very important tool you'll need: a hunting slingshot. Mine is an old Wham-O; I got it when I was a kid in the '50s.

Now, on with the drive. First, survey the area from a distance, and select a close vantage point that gives you a good view of the thick cover. A topo map can help you locate such a spot if you don't know the area well.

Walking around the cover rather than through it, go to a spot that's directly opposite the vantage point. Make some noise as you approach, but don't sound like a bulldozer. Stay at the edge of the cover, 10 to 20 yards away from the thick stuff.

Once you're at the spot opposite the vantage point, start a two-way conversation with yourself, at a normal tone of voice. Do this for a couple of minutes. Now walk in one direction along the edge; don't try to be silent as you walk. After a short time, stop and sneak back to the starting spot, being careful not to make any noise. Once you're back to the starting point, walk in the other direction, making some noise as you go.

By this time, "the Big Boy" is fully alerted to your presence, and thinks there are two hunters out there. The buck will be intent on the "creatures" doing the walking and talking.

At this point, sneak quietly around the thick cover to the predetermined vantage point as quickly as you can. When you reach this area, set yourself up and get out your slingshot. Find some small- to medium-sized stones; round ones are best as they seem to make the right sound.

Now, let the games begin! Start lobbing stones—not too many, nor too fast—toward the edge of the heavy cover where you did the walking and talking. Your first stones should land on the outside edge of that cover, as close to your starting point as possible. Start working the stones inward toward your current location … slowly, as though someone is walking toward you. Be on guard, for now the buck thinks you and your friend are coming in the front door. Being the cautious creature that he is, he's now going to sneak out the back door … yep, right where you are.

This has worked for me on many occasions. I figure you don't have much to lose by trying it, because if you went into the cover one way the buck would just slip out the other. Also, if things get slow, you can take potshots at those pesky bushytails without shooting them … something to do while waiting for the whitetail action to pick up!

John Katinas
Bellerose, NY

Pay Attention to Wind Direction

In my 20-plus years of hunting experience, I have learned that the greatest obstacle to overcome in hunting most big game (deer especially) is their amazing sense of smell. There are many scents available on the market to help overcome this problem. I have tried many of them. Some have worked to a degree and some have failed miserably. None have proved to completely deceive a deer's ability to detect even the slightest hint of human odor.

There is one method, however, that is effective in overcoming this problem when done properly: always hunt with the wind in your face. When still-hunting, I always choose my direction of travel so the prevailing wind is either crosswise or directly in my face. When stand-hunting, determine the prevailing wind direction and likely game approach routes, then position your stand so it is downwind of the route the game will move.

Before leaving my house to go hunting, I always listen to the weather radio to hear the current wind direction, as well as the forecast direction for the remainder of the day. In my area, this information is correct most of the time. I also check the wind direction when leaving my vehicle to enter the woods. I use this information in conjunction with a map of my hunting area to determine the best approach to my chosen stand or still-hunting area.

Robert Holmberg
LaPine, AL

THE EXPERT'S NOTEBOOK

How to Fool Late-Season Birds ... by Chris Winchester

When hunting waterfowl late in the season after all the small ponds and lakes have iced up, you can make a "fake opening" in a frozen-over pond to attract birds. Here's how.

Pour 5 to 10 gallons of water on top of the ice; you can use an auger to drill a hole through the ice if it's more convenient than carrying water. Place duck and goose shell decoys around the edges of the water and get ready.

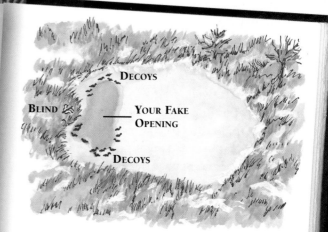

The water will look like an open pocket for passing birds to land in.

This trick is especially effective for late-season mallards and Canada geese.

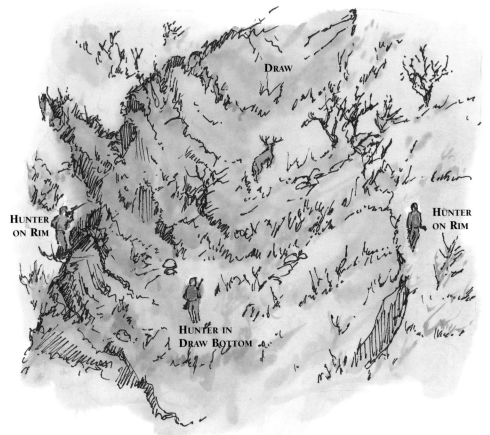

DRAW

HUNTER
ON RIM

HUNTER
ON RIM

HUNTER IN
DRAW BOTTOM

quick tip

Deer Drives: Squirt-Out Points

The term "deer drive" is a misnomer. It's more like a "deer move" because that's about all you can really do, if you can even do that. If a whitetail is going to move at all, it is going to go where *the deer* wants to go, and that's not necessarily straight ahead.

So when I move deer, my stander(s) are as likely to be to the sides or maybe even in back of the cover I am working, as they are to be in front. It seems logical to have someone in front, but that's seldom where the deer go. So cover the "squirt-out" points, those oddball places deer *really* use to escape moving hunter(s).

*Tom Carpenter
Plymouth, MN*

Hunt All Day

We hunt mulies in a western area that is borderline desert. Sagebrush is the tallest vegetation available in the area.

Many of the local hunters spend the first hour and last hour of daylight glassing, spending the rest of the day at home. We glass those hours also, but instead of giving up, we walk the draws for the rest of the day.

Bucks hold really tight and it is common to "bust" one to four mule deer bucks at 40 to 60 yards. The trick is to walk *every* bit of cover, especially the benches at the top of side draws.

The system works great with three hunters—one walking each rim of a draw and one walking the bottom. Action isn't steady, but when it comes, it's fast and furious

with only a few seconds to decide if a buck is big enough and then to get a clean, killing shot. If the first to run is a spike, we've learned to be on the lookout since mulies are still in bachelor groups during most hunting seasons.

When doing this sort of walk, safety should be your number one concern. No matter how excited you may get when a muley bursts from cover, you must be absolutely certain that your shot is safe. Know exactly where your partners are at all times.

Last tip: If you're on public land, don't expect bucks to stop and look back at you! Those bucks are all dead.

*Philip Stewart
Liverpool, NY*

Set Up to Ambush Spring Turkeys

I have hunted turkeys each spring for 15 years, and although I've had a high success rate, it is more due to the quantity of birds in the area than my hunting prowess. As I became more experienced, I recognized that the ambush setup was critical to success.

Each year I begin by going into turkey territory about three weeks prior to the season. My goal is to locate the roosting areas and pattern the birds' habits after they come off the roosts. There is such a tremendous amount of wildlife movement in early spring, and I find that after being cooped up all winter, this renewal of life is exhilarating. I have had many wonderful wildlife experiences during these forays, and my camcorder has provided a record I'll always cherish.

Turkeys aren't rigid creatures of habit, so habitat dictates movements to feeding and breeding areas. There always seem to be two or three routes available when the birds come off the roost, but they will take

one of these more consistently than the others. Weather can be a factor in the birds' movements as well. High wind, rain or snow will cause the birds to vary the time they come off the roost and the direction in which they travel. In each case, an ambush setup must be pre-located, which will offer the opportunity to bag this most wily of birds.

In the ideal ambush location, the birds will pass close enough to you when they're leaving the roost to be called in to your decoys, even when the tom has hens alongside. The spot you choose to sit in should provide good long-range vision to both sides as well as in front, with enough cover to allow you to bring up your weapon well in advance of the birds coming into range. Avoid a location where the birds can surprise you from the rear. My favorite spots have heavy brush behind my position, and the turkeys can't get through the tangle.

Since you may be in this location for several hours, comfort is important. A cushion to sit on helps greatly. Lean against a large tree, and make sure you can move your legs to keep circulation going.

Over the years, I have developed three locations that fit this criteria, and I've been very successful in all three spots. I have used hen decoys or a combination of hen and jake decoys, and have even hunted with no decoys at all. I find the combination to be most effective. Developing your calling skills is also critical. My favorite is the plain ol' box call.

Get out early in spring, do your field work (or rather, "woods work"), and find good locations where you can set up to ambush the wily turkey.

Raymond McDaniel
Linden, WI

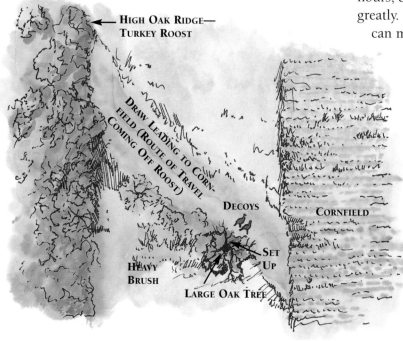

HIGH OAK RIDGE—
TURKEY ROOST

DRAW LEADING TO CORN-
FIELD (ROUTE OF TRAVEL
COMING OFF ROOST)

DECOYS

CORNFIELD

SET
UP

HEAVY
BRUSH

LARGE OAK TREE

FROM THE EXPERT'S NOTEBOOK

Waterfowling Tips... by Chris Winchester

-When geese are coming toward you, always shoot at the rear of the flock first and work your way forward. This will help avoid causing all the birds to flare out of range before you get a follow-up shot.

-When scouting for geese after spotting a feeding flock, wait for them to leave, then set up exactly where they were earlier. You should not need large numbers of decoys when doing this. Be careful not to disturb or alarm the geese while they are feeding.

-If pass-shooting geese, allow the first couple of flocks to pass over without shooting. This will, in turn, make the trailing flocks less wary, and they will fly lower.

-If a pair or small flock of geese come in and you shoot one or two, start to call immediately. More often than not, you can turn the mate and get a second chance. Geese mate for life and will often come back to see where their mate has gone.

CHRIS WINCHESTER

A Different Bear Bait

Instead of the traditional "jelly doughnut," try dog food at your bear baiting station. Buy the cheap dry stuff in 50-pound bags and spice it up by mixing in bacon grease and meat drippings.

Michael C. Thompson
Border, AK

quick tip

Confidence Decoys

When using a blind stand by a waterhole, set a few goose decoys by the water. Geese have excellent eyesight and their presence calms big game animals.

Jeremy Evers
Burns, OR

Muzzleloader Adventure on NAHC-Won Hunt

Anticipation and excitement traveled with us as my good huntin' buddy, Rich, and I left home early that May morning. We were heading for New Brunswick, Canada, to meet outfitter/guide Clarence Walton, owner-operator of Henderson's Hunting Camp, for a black bear hunt I had won through the NAHC membership drive. We arrived early Sunday evening anticipating a special week since all the hunters in camp would be NAHC members.

This type of hunt was new to me, so I had many questions and wanted to learn as much as possible. I'd spoken with Clarence often over the past months and had gotten much advice about the upcoming hunt. I had brought along my new Knight T-Bolt 50-cal. muzzleloader; I had been very impressed with the Knight muzzleloaders after shooting them at the last two Jamborees and talking with Tony Knight. I would be shooting 150 grains of Pyrodex powder, pushing a 300-grain Barnes X bullet.

Clarence met us at the door of the lodge with introductions all around. His prediction for the week's hunt was good, but he was concerned because the weather had been unseasonably warm. It had been near 90°F, and everything was blooming, even the fiddlehead ferns. Clarence explained that bears love ferns, and will gorge themselves on them to purge their systems from their long winter's sleep. The bears hadn't stopped coming in to the baits, but there had been a slowdown.

Clarence told me that he had a pristine spot picked out for me—a ground blind on the edge of an area that had been logged a few years earlier. He asked if I was up to it, as he knew I would be using a muzzleloader. My reply was: absolutely, that's what I'm here for—the excitement and adventure.

We drove across the town, potato fields and a stream and, finally, down the logging road near where I'd be hunting. When we stopped, Clarence said, "Look down there in the mud on the side of

the road." I did, and saw bear tracks. He proceeded to spray me down with essence of fall cover scent. I grabbed my smokepole and we were off.

Clarence had me go first in case we came across a bear. After a quarter-mile walk, the clearing was just ahead, and we approached slowly. No bear was in sight, but there were enough tracks to keep the adrenaline going. Clarence went ahead and checked the bait barrel, which hadn't been touched. Then he got me settled in the blind. As he left, he gave me words of encouragement: "Remember, they'll probably come out over by the bait. Keep an eye out behind, though; there is at least a 300-pounder working this area." Then he quietly disappeared.

Squirrels, ravens and ducks kept me awake until darkness began to set in. As I left my blind,

As smoke drifted back into my face, I couldn't believe my eyes. Three more bears walked out right where the one I had shot disappeared. Was I dreaming?

thoughts flashed through my head. Did I move around too much or make too much noise? No, I couldn't have. I was too excited, especially since it was the first day. Suddenly headlights flashed ahead of me; it was Clarence. So far, none of the guys he'd seen yet had gotten a bear.

We headed out to pick up Butch, who was waiting at the pickup spot with a half smile. "I'm sure I got off a good shot, but the bear disappeared in the thick stuff." Off we went into the darkness to track Butch's possible downed bear. Clarence held the only real flashlight, while Butch and I had our little mini Mag-Lites. That was an interesting experience, not knowing what we were walking up on—a dead bear, a wounded bear, or maybe just a plain ol' hungry bear! "Here's where he was; there's where he went," said Butch.

We searched around in the darkness but saw no sign of a hit. Down a trail went Clarence, and when he had gone about 30 feet, he hollered back, "Here it is!" Butch had made a quick, clean kill. It was a young bear about 2 to 3 years old. Butch was happy!

Days two and three brought the same results. Up to now Butch was the only hunter to see a bear.

All of us were losing a bit of our edge. Clarence and the guides kept up the encouragement, and took some of us out in the mornings while they freshened up the baits and opened some new ones.

As the fourth day's hunt started, I settled into my blind a little disheartened but still content with the knowledge that good things happen for those who are patient and wait. I did become a little careless and decided to take a smoke break after eating a sandwich (hey! the wind was in my face!). So I lit one up, turned my head to the left and wham, there it was—*a bear!* It had been walking up the logging road, and now was ambling into the brush just off the road. Suddenly there was another behind the first one. They both disappeared into the brush. I'd see black movement and then I wouldn't. My eyes were straining, hoping I'd catch a clear opening. Then, nothing.

Forever passed—probably just seconds—then suddenly, just halfway to the bait, there was a bear standing on a dirt mound, quartering away. My mind raced … "It's definitely an adult, it's getting towards dusk, fourth day, only one more chance possibly … yep, this is the one!" I settled my sight behind the right shoulder: "…mid-body, a little higher, take both lungs, not too high, long hair, break the opposite shoulder …" *Pow!* A cloud of smoke, and the bear disappeared.

As smoke drifted back into my face, I couldn't believe my eyes, and thought I was dreaming. Three more bears walked out right where mine had disappeared. Again my mind raced. No, I wasn't dreaming; there were three bears right in front of me, my shot hadn't scared them off. I looked for red, a limp, a stumble; no, there were three different bears right in front of me.

The seconds passed, and suddenly one of the three started coming toward me, shaking its head from side to side, not looking real friendly. No! I thought, it's not the time to stand still and hope he doesn't see me, that's already happened. "Powder, down the barrel … bullet from shirt pocket (I'll bet I shoved that bullet halfway down the barrel with my thumb) … ramrod, finish setting the bullet … capper, on the nipple, cock it … I'm ready." Now the stare down. I didn't move, didn't blink, I'm not sure if I was even breathing yet.

When the bear was about twelve yards away, it turned suddenly and joined the other two. Whew! I finally started breathing again. I settled down on my makeshift seat and watched as the three browsed around the clearing for the next fifteen minutes.

Finally, two of the three walked over to where they had entered the clearing; one walked partway up the dirt mound and looked over. Yeah! He's checking out my bear that's right where it should be. Then the two vanished into the brush. The third bear moseyed over to the bait barrel, reached over and took a bag of stale donuts off the top and stood perfectly broadside. Oh oh! This baby's back is as high as that 55-gallon drum. I know he's big. Bigger

Continued …

than the one I shot at? I wasn't sure, but I thought so. Again my mind raced. I had already settled my sights on his shoulder, but nope, hunting ethics took over. I had made my shot. Even though I didn't see or hear my bear go down, I was sure I'd had a good shot. Ease up, buddy! You already have yours. Then the big bruiser vanished into the brush.

It was getting near dark, and now that the bears were gone, it was time for me to get out of there and cover the half-mile to where I was to meet Clarence. I started down the logging road, but something made me look back. Oh oh! Here comes big brother, on the lope across the clearing, and not looking as if he was coming over to congratulate me. I turned and faced him, rifle ready.

We hunters need to be not only skilled but knowledgeable in how and what we do.

The bear stopped at forty yards, hair standing on end (so was mine). The bear stood up on its hind feet and threw its head from side to side trying to catch my scent. I had a big mudhole behind me. I didn't want to turn and fall while trying to hop through it, so I knelt on one knee and braced for a good shot if I needed to take it. The bruin dropped to all fours, took three steps closer, clacked his teeth twice, threw his head sideways and up, gave a guttural grunt and walked into the brush. Now I'm no fool! I was sure he was telling me "This is my home and you better leave." A second suggestion wasn't necessary; I was out of there.

It didn't take me long to get out to the pickup spot, looking over my shoulder all the way. I pulled the hunter orange ribbon from the tree, a signal to Clarence that I needed help. I stood for a second and thought, what am I standing here for, with all this brush and trees around me, so I headed out into the open potato field. I no sooner got out there and I could see the headlights from Clarence's truck.

Clarence jumped out all excited. "Did ya?" "Yep," I said, "let's go get 'em." As we bounced along back to the clearing, Clarence asked a million questions. I answered, but I was so excited I wasn't sure I was making any sense. Clarence stopped

where the road hit the opening, and we both jumped out into the near darkness. Clarence grabbed his flashlight and ax, and I had my muzzleloader. "Ya got full load in 'er?" Clarence asked. "Yep." Now where was the bear?

As we approached the dirt mound, we could see the bear's tracks and the claw marks it made after the shot. We searched and searched but found no hair and no blood. "Are you sure you had a good shot?" "Absolutely! It was wide open!" Clarence and I went into the darkness of the undergrowth. "Stay right on my tail," Clarence said as he ranged the light back and forth. Suddenly he stopped. "Do you hear that?" The other bears were moving around in the darkness. "It's going to be a clear, cold night, and this is not the best place to be right now. We'll come back and find him in the morning."

I spent the night replaying my shot over and over in my mind. The next morning, five of us loaded into Clarence's van. Regrettably, I hadn't thought of taking the muzzleloader. Clarence handed me a short double-barreled 12 gauge in case we got in close quarters and the bear wasn't finished. We arrived at the clearing and all examined the area again, this time in the sunlight. Still no blood, no hair. We went back through the whole scene again, and then fanned out a few yards apart. We took our time searching—for anything, for something—but still nothing. We had gone in about 40 yards and over to my right I heard Clarence talking to Rich. "I think Earl missed him clean." Then Clarence came over by me and repeated the same thing to me.

Those words no sooner hit my ear when Jimmy and Butch urgently whispered, "Get over here—we found him." The sow (yes, "he" turned out to be "she") was approximately seven to eight years old and weighed about 180 pounds. Well, I'll tell ya I'm happy. You're doggone right I'm happy.

We cut a strong pole, tied the bear to it, and carried it the rest of the way to the van. When we got there we laid the bear out on a dirt mound and the cameras came out. We took lots of pictures with lots of smiles. I regret I didn't think to bring the muzzleloader, as it would have made a perfect picture of a great hunting adventure.

When the rolls of film were finished off, we went to the butcher. The initial autopsy revealed that my bullet had entered just behind the right shoulder mid-body, had caught the front portion of the right lung, somehow missed the left lung, busted the left shoulder, and exited.

I know the bear was quartering away, but I should have held five inches farther back and the job would have been finished.

The best part of the situation was that we were able to recover my bear and thus able to determine that I could have made a little better shot. Well, that's how we learn, and we as hunters have that obligation, not only to our quarry, but to each other, and to all the non-hunters. As we pick up little pieces of information like this, we become more efficient and skilled hunters. In these days and times, we hunters need to be not only skilled, but knowledgeable, in how and what we do.

I would like to express my appreciation to the North American Hunting Club for the chance to go on this trip, and to Clarence and Stephanie Walton of Henderson's Hunting Camps for the donated hunt.

Earl H. Biller
Chicago, IL

SPECIAL EXPERT ADVICE

quick tip

Dry Turkey Calls

While turkey hunting in the rain may not be very comfortable, it can be productive. But rain can quickly silence friction calls such as boxes and slates, if they get very wet.

Carry several gallon-sized zip-top plastic bags in your turkey vest or jacket. If it starts to rain, put your friction calls in the bag. Not only will the bag protect the calls when they're not in use, but when you want to sound off with your box call, you can operate it without ever taking it out of the bag. The call will stay dry and continue to sound authentic throughout your rainy-day hunt.

Glenn Sapir
Shrub Oak, NY

THE EXPERT'S NOTEBOOK

Walk Like a Deer ... by Mark Kayser

Instead of walking into the woods in a typical plodding human fashion, I copy the pace and style of a deer's movements. I learned this tactic by watching unalerted deer from my stand and seeing how they react to deer approaching them. Deer step lightly and purposefully, plus they stop every few steps and re-evaluate their surroundings for danger. By copying this approach, I spook fewer deer while going to my stand, and it allows me to get closer to deer when still-hunting and calling. I've increased my success this way.

quick tip

Two for Antelope

I have two tips I use when antelope hunting.

First, when approaching the top of a grassy hill, start looking through the grass rather than over it. Many times I have been able to spot the white of an antelope through the grass while avoiding being spotted by the antelope.

Second, when judging trophy-quality, I like to see the base of the prong above the tip of the ear. I have found this to be the general starting point for antelope in the 13- to 14-inch class.

Nathan S. Gilbertson
Breckenridge, MN

A Natural Mule Deer "Decoy"

I had taken a stand in my favorite Wyoming woods one season at about 5:50 a.m. About ten minutes later, a muley doe bedded down about 75 yards away from me, to my left front quarter. My first thought was, "I wish she'd leave." My second thought was, "Hey, what a great decoy!"

I was standing with my back to a pine tree, between the doe and the eventual sun. The temperature was about 50°F, and the sun would be coming up over my right shoulder. The doe spent most of the time watching me, but now and then would direct attention elsewhere. During these times, I lifted my rifle barrel slowly to keep the rising sun from shining on it.

At about 6:50 a.m. I heard a twig or stick break about 200 yards away to my right front quarter. Several does and fawns started a single-file parade 30 to 40 yards in front of me, moving toward the bedded doe. A few minutes later, I saw two bucks walking toward the does, following the exact trail taken by the does.

The bucks had their heads to the ground most of the time, and seemed unaware of my presence. About 75 yards from me, there was a small dip in the ground. When the biggest of the two bucks reached this dip, I was unable to see the buck's head, but the rest of the body was visible. I figured this was my chance, and took my shot and dropped the buck in its tracks.

The lesson here is to take advantage of the situation. That original doe gave the other deer a sense of confidence, enabling me to get an easy shot on a fine buck.

Vernon Denzer
Dane, WI

My Favorite Waterfowl Tips

Here are some tips for waterfowling enthusiasts:

- Wrap your shotshell boxes in duct tape. This not only adds strength, it helps repel water.
- While goose hunting with my 3½-inch 12 gauge shotgun, I stagger my shells in this order: 2¾-inch, 3-inch, and finally 3½-inch. The theory is that the geese should be closest on the first shot, requiring less velocity and less shot. Also, the 2¾-inch shell requires a much shorter throw than the longer shells, making for a much quicker second shot. The third shell is saved for those departing shots when the geese are leaving range. This method has resulted in many, many more "doubles" and even the occasional "triple."
- When using field decoys on cold mornings, be sure to keep a rag handy and use it to wipe the frost off the decoys. A little frost can go a long way in affecting the believability of your set. Brass-based hulls are also a warning for wary geese, and will cause them to flare.

Jeremy Evers
Burns, OR

FROM THE EXPERT'S NOTEBOOK

Pheasant Hunting Tips... by Jim Van Norman

Here's a tip that will help you harvest more smart, long-tailed roosters. In the "olden days" when I was taught to hunt pheasants by my father and grandfather, one thing that would earn a stern look from either man was talking while on a pheasant drive. Pheasants have extremely good hearing and learn to associate human voices with big trouble. Granted, you make plenty of noise while traversing heavy cover, but the pheasants don't know if you're a cow, a deer, a horse or what. But let one human voice be heard and pheasants know to "get out of town!" Plan some simple hand signals with your hunting partners and keep voices to a minimum. Use whistles to handle your dogs when possible. Save the high fives and hollering until the end of the drive.

Another tip for outsmarting old long-tailed roosters: Carry a hawk whistle. As you are working a patch of cover, blow the hawk call every now and then. Pheasants will hold better instead of making a run for it. And while hunting heavy cover, don't just walk at a steady pace; vary it considerably and stop dead in your tracks regularly. When a predator such as a fox or coyote is hunting pheasants in cover and they spot a bird, they freeze for a moment just before they leap. Pheasants know this well and when you stop suddenly in cover, a bird that is holding tight will think, "The jig's up" and may flush immediately. This tactic stops many of those wily roosters from letting you walk by and then flushing, or just walking away after you pass.

quick tip

Tricking Snowshoe Hares

There are a lot of snow-shoe hares where I live, and I frequently hunt them. Sometimes as I lift my rifle up to take a shot, a hare will bolt into the surrounding brush for cover. If I lose sight of the hare, I scratch lightly at the checkering on the stock of my rifle. These animals are notorious for sitting perfectly still for extended amounts of time, but the noise from the scratching makes them flick their ears ever so slightly. Most of the time, this flicking is just enough to give away their position. I have been rather successful with this trick.

Michael C. Thompson
Border, AK

Turkey Hunting 101

April turkey season … my first hunt! I had read everything I could find about turkey hunting and watched all the films on TV. I purchased a box call and a dia-phragm call, and drove our dog half-crazy practicing! I was ready.

Opening Morning. I heard a turkey gobble. I walked up to within 100 yards of the sound and sat with my back to a tree, just like all the films I had watched. Every time I called, the turkey answered back. In my mind's eye, I could see the bird strutting back and forth, because every time it called, the sound came from a different spot in front of me.

After almost an hour of this, I still hadn't seen the turkey. I had a bright idea: Why not sneak up closer on my stomach? I've been able to sneak within bow range of pronghorn antelope, so why not a turkey? Mistake #1.

I had crawled about ten yards when three toms flew away from three different trees. Mistake #2: I didn't realize it, but the birds were still roosted. It was 9:00 a.m. and they had been sitting in tall pine trees watching until I got too close. Everything I had read said that turkeys fly down at dawn, but these didn't.

Day Two. I walked for two hours but never heard a thing. When I got back to my truck, I heard a gobble about 50 yards away. I sat down and started calling. I heard a hen call to my right; the tom was answering the hen as well as my call. After what seemed like hours of dueling what I thought was a hen, a shot rang out. Mistake #3.

Day Three. Called up another hen. Where were all the toms?

Day Four. Forgot my head net. Called to a tom at the bottom of a ridge until he walked out of range.

Day Five. Tried to sneak up on another tom. End of day five, and also the end of me sneaking up on turkeys. I finished my first season without firing a shot.

April turkey season … my second season. I went to a turkey seminar, bought new calls and practiced, practiced, practiced until I was ready. Arkansas has a long season, and I went out every day it wasn't raining.

Many more mistakes were made. It was the next-to-last day of the season, and I still hadn't gotten my gobbler. I was walking down a trail and calling every so often. About 10:00 a.m. I heard a tom double-gobble at the bottom of a hill. I stepped off the trail about ten feet, sat with my back to a tree and called twice. The tom double-gobbled again. I brought my shotgun up and made ready so when the bird came into sight I wouldn't have to move. When the tom raised his head, I shot, and I missed!

With the shot, a flock of turkeys I hadn't even seen were flying everywhere. I picked the first tom I could identify, fired and had my limit within seconds. Turkey hunting is easy, isn't it?!

Robert Krause
Mountain Home, AR

A Mountaintop Hunt for Trophy Mule Deer

Hunting big mulies challenges a hunter not only physically, but mentally as well. For more than 25 years I've traveled across the country to hunt Colorado public land in search of big mulies. In that time, I've taken five record-book bucks, including the #1 in the first edition of the Longhunter Muzzleloading Record Book. Two hunting partners (my brother, Jack, and my nephew, Gary) have taken several record-book bucks also. But don't get me wrong; big mulies are as hard to kill as they are to locate.

One of the best ways to find a good area with big bucks is to look through record books from the Boone and Crockett or Pope and Young clubs and The Longhunter Society. Check to see what areas have produced the greatest number of record-book trophies.

Next, contact other hunters and ranchers who have been around the area. It doesn't matter how good a hunter you are, you can't take a big muley if they're not there.

Most of our hunting is done in or around September. This is a great time because big mulies are usually high up on the mountains in September. I usually hunt between 8,000 and 9,500 feet. It's not an easy climb, but it's one of the hardships you must bear to get near big bucks.

Scouting the area for a few days before the season is a good idea, but don't get too close because if you spook a buck or leave scent, you may cause the buck to disappear for the season. Instead, I prefer glassing with binoculars or a spotting scope from a long distance, usually on the south side of a mountain. Many of the big bucks I eventually took were spotted this way.

Once you locate a good buck on a mountain, it becomes a matter of getting within killing distance. Still-hunting is effective, but the country is so big that you can't hunt too slowly or the whole day will pass before you have time to find your buck. One of the techniques we use to help in this situation is to have two hunters work their way toward each other from opposite ends of the mountain. This can cause an old, smart buck to make a mistake and be pushed toward one of the hunters. We've also placed a hunter in a good location near the top—maybe in a notch—so a hunter working in front may push a buck to the waiting hunter at the top.

The largest buck I ever killed was taken using two of these techniques. I spotted the buck the day before the season from a half-mile away. It was with two smaller bucks, and they moved up into some aspen near the top of the mountain.

Three of us were there the next morning at daybreak, but the mountainside was covered with domestic sheep and there was not a deer to be found. Mule deer and sheep don't share the same areas; usually the deer move out until the sheep are gone. Luckily the sheep moved on later that afternoon, so my brother Jack and I decided to hunt the evening there.

Jack went about three-quarters of the way up the mountain, while I climbed the back side and was hunting from the top. Jack jumped the monster buck below me, but got only a glimpse of it. The buck came straight to me, and after I shot it I couldn't believe my eyes. With a 30-inch spread and 14-inch front Y's, this 187⅞ buck was the largest on record ever taken with a muzzleloader. Big mulies are tough to come by, but when you get a good one, it's a hunt you'll never forget.

Tom Garvin
Rising Sun, MD

Take Advantage of the Situation

A recent deer season in the Blue Mountains of Washington State found me eight yards from a feeding 4-point muley carrying a 22-inch spread. Many tips and strategies, as well as some luck, went into that hunt to get me in that position. But the most important tip I can offer is this: When you're in the woods, you're hunting! Always position yourself to take advantage of what the situation might provide.

I had hunted hard for six full days without much positive feedback. I'd seen some small bucks, but the game unit I was hunting had a 3-point-per-side minimum. After sitting stand until 10:00 a.m. with no sightings, I had to move out of boredom and frustration with the heat. I started a circular hunt down a ridge and back. Soon the morning coffee was calling to me, so I looked for a place to conduct nature's business. I walked over to an embankment and looked down into a thicket as I began to relieve myself. Movement caught my eye, and I refocused to notice a very large mule deer right below me. I raised my .30-06 and fired with my business end still hanging out of my pants.

If I had not taken every opportunity to place myself in a position where I could see, I would have missed this fine buck. Hunting is about being in the right place at the right time. Don't limit yourself; position yourself!

Chris Tennant
Pullman, WA

WAYS WITH WEAPONS

When a rooster pheasant bursts from the cover at your feet, does your shotgun come smoothly and effortlessly to your shoulder, or do you have to think about what you're doing? Are you confident about your aim when you have a buck in your sights? Can you judge wind strength and adjust to make an accurate bow shot?

This chapter's ideas help you polish your skills with all types of weapons. From at-home practice techniques, to proven field tips, to the psychology of shooting, you are sure to pick up some new and helpful ways with weapons.

Never Too Old to Learn

You hear many stories about bucks being shot on Halloween. Mine has a little different twist.

My father has hunted small game since he was five or six years old. Often, it was to get food for the family; sometimes he traded rabbits for groceries or for more shells to hunt with. Later, a love for being in the woods and for hunting got him interested in upland game. So when deer first returned to our part of Illinois, he was ready to try his luck.

The first deer season in our county was in the mid-'70s. For the next few years, my father hunted the two weekends of slug season, killing a few deer for us to eat.

Several years later I took up bowhunting. I would relate my experiences to my father, as he was always curious to know if I had seen or killed a deer. After a few years, Dad told me that if he could shoot a bow he'd like to try it. We bought him a used bow because he wasn't sure he'd be able to draw when the weather turned colder, due to his arthritis. After trying a few shots, he didn't think he could shoot well enough to kill a deer. My dad hates to see any animal suffer and always strives for a clean kill. So he sold the bow.

The following summer, after talking to me and a few friends, he decided to try again. So we bought another bow, turned down the poundage and started showing him how to judge yardage and shoot correctly. After a month of practice, he felt comfortable with the bow, and confident that he could kill a deer at close range. I

gave him an old climbing tree-stand that he welded up solid. I also gave him a grunt call.

The season started on October 1, but arthritis and other things kept him out of the stand. He did ride his three-wheeler around looking for deer sign and telling me what he'd seen. The week before Halloween he used the three-wheeler to carry the old deer stand to a tree he'd picked out. On Halloween morning, Dad took the bow to the hunting site. After climbing the tree and getting settled in, he blew the grunt call and waited. After five or ten minutes, he gave a couple more grunts, and saw a deer coming his way. A nice 8-point buck walked through 20 yards in front of my dad, looking for an intruder. That's how it happened that at 70 years of age, Dad got his first archery buck.

While he was waiting to begin tracking, he noticed movement to his left and saw a big 10-point coming to investigate. He watched the buck pass by at 30 yards. He was both happy with his luck and wishing he had another buck tag!

This story shows that you are never too old to try something new. Also, you don't have to spend a lot of money on top-of-the-line products. Used archery equipment is cheap and it allows you to find out if this is a sport you want to pursue. The main thing is to get someone to help you get properly set up, and practice until you are confident you can make a clean kill.

Steve Slater
Salem, IL

FROM THE EXPERT'S NOTEBOOK

Truly Clean Barrels...by Ron Spomer

Most hunters know that microscopic burrs and cracks in barrels peel metal from bullets. When these elements combine with layers of powder ash, the buildup squeezes and deforms bullets, reducing accuracy. Some smooth barrels remain accurate for dozens of rounds, rough ones might not make it to ten, but eventually all must be cleaned in order to restore their former glory. Unfortunately, few shooters understand how to get a barrel really clean.

Until I examined a rifle barrel through a Hawkeye magnifying borescope, I didn't realize just what it takes to get one absolutely clean. What looked perfect and shiny to my naked eye proved to be coated with bullet jacket material. Only after repeated applications of various solvents and brushes did I discover how to scrub a bore whistling clean. Here's the trick:

1. Use a one-piece rod and wipe it clean after every few passes down the bore to remove abrasive dirt.

2. Use a boreguide to center the rod and protect rifling.

3. Use loop tip, not cut tip, nylon or brass brushes. Most copper-removing solvents erode brass, so I like nylon. Stainless steel is too hard.

4. Cover scope lenses so solvent overspray doesn't etch the expensive glass.

5. Wrap a patch around the brush. Saturate it with one of the copper-stripping solvents available at sporting goods stores. Push through bore. Remove the patch/brush at muzzle and pull rod back through. Let sit 15 minutes.

6. Run another saturated patch through. Let sit 5 to 10 minutes. This softens accumulated gunk.

7. Smear JB Compound (a mildly abrasive cleaning paste used by benchrest shooters and sold by Brownell's) on a patch/brush. Push and pull this through the bore ten times.

8. Push a saturated patch through, followed by 2 or 3 dry patches to remove lose gunk.

9. Repeat steps 6 and 7 but increase strokes to 50.

10. Repeat step 8. At this point, a relatively smooth barrel should be clean. Rough ones might need another 50 polishing strokes with the JB. Always finish with a wet patch or two and enough dry patches to remove all moisture.

11. Lastly, pass an oiled patch down the bore to seal the metal from rust. Apply a relatively heavy coat if storing the gun for any length of time and remember to run a dry patch through to remove excess oil before shooting.

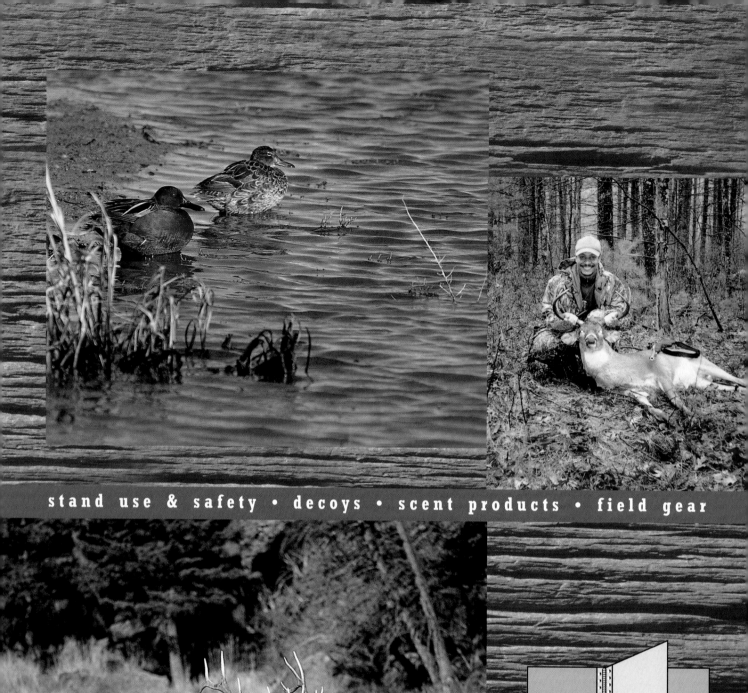

EQUIPMENT ESSENTIALS

Every hunter picks up little techniques and tricks to get the most use out of equipment, increase hunting efficiency and make time spent afield more enjoyable.

Whether it's a way to salvage old decoys, ideas for customizing gear or suggestions for items you should consider putting into your pack, you'll find a wealth of helpful suggestions and advice in this chapter ... all geared toward increasing your hunting enjoyment.

Glowsticks Help in Tracking

When hunting in the evening, I always make sure I have a few "glowsticks" (also known as Cyalume lightsticks) with me. Blood trails are sometimes hard to follow even in daylight, and can be even more difficult when darkness falls.

Glowsticks have helped me several times while I was tracking deer. I always have at least two of them with me when I am starting on a blood trail; three is even better since it lets you see the "line" the deer is taking.

I place a glowstick where I find blood, and use it as a reference when looking for the next spot of blood. When I find the next one, I place the second glowstick on it and go back for the first one. I continue to leapfrog in this manner without having to waste time trying to re-find the last blood, or worry about losing it altogether. We all know how easy it is to get turned around in the woods when your nose is to the ground looking for blood.

Glowsticks are also very helpful when you lose the blood trail and have to do a circular search around the spot where you saw the last blood. Just hang the glowstick in a tree over the last blood and you will be able to see the light from a great distance.

I have found yellow and white to be the brightest colors; and once, when my flashlight batteries ran low and I had to go back to my truck for more, I saw my glowsticks in the woods from more than 250 yards away when I was coming back. Needless to say, I got back to the blood trail with no problems.

The cheapest glowsticks I have found are from Crawford Tools, 101 TDK Boulevard, Peachtree City, GA 30269; 800-272-9373.

I hope you find this tip useful. It really has helped me stay on track when the light is failing.

Frank Kendall
Portage, IN

THE EXPERT'S NOTEBOOK

Watch That Face ... by Bob Robb

Bowhunters know how their shiny faces and hands can glare like headlights in the night, spooking game no matter how well the rest of their bodies and equipment are camouflaged. Savvy waterfowl hunters know this too. They camouflage their own shiny faces with either a mesh face mask or camo face paint, and also wear dark or camo gloves on their hands. These measures keep ducks and geese from flaring at the sight of those little beacons of light in a sea of marshland cover.

Toy Decoys for Predator Hunting

While predator hunting one cool morning in Oklahoma with a friend who is a long-time predator hunting veteran, we were talking about decoys. Being new to the sport, I listened as he told me that a rabbit decoy would get the predator an extra few yards closer to my position, increasing my chances for a successful shot.

Well, this sounded good to me; but the problem was, none of the retailers in the surrounding area sold anything like that. I didn't want to mail-order a decoy, because I didn't want to wait that long. So I went to a local store that sold stuffed animals, and bought a toy rabbit. Now mind you, it didn't look like the real thing, but the basic shape was there. I took it out the very next day and could not believe the success rate I gained from that one little tip. Now that I've been hunting predators for a few years, I've got some tips of my own that just might help you out:

- When using a decoy for predators, always face it away from you. Try to face it upwind if possible, because most predators like to come in from the downwind side.
- I've also learned to always carry a spare decoy.
- I carry a ball of twine, about 30 yards long, especially when I am bowhunting. I tie the twine somewhere low on the decoy and string it back to my blind. This provides me with a good yardage indicator, and also helps in other ways you might not have thought of. I've had hawks

swoop in and try to take my decoy, and with the twine I can pull it back quickly rather than watching my decoy take flight. I learned this the hard way!

- I've had success with several different types of stuffed animals, from rabbits to dogs. Anything that gets a predator's attention away from you will help.
- Predators have very keen eyesight, so it's important to suit up completely in camo, and to keep movement to a minimum.
- A cover scent such as coon or fox urine also helps prevent the predator from finding you. I even put a little scent around the decoy.
- Park at least 100 yards from your hunting spot, because predators don't like to come in near a vehicle.
- Try not to use the same stand or blind every time you hunt predators, because they soon learn that this spot means danger and will avoid it.

I hope these tips help you out on your next hunt. Good luck, and good hunting!

Chris Hughes
Sayre, OK

Two Ways to Make Your Own Acorn Scent

For an authentic and strong acorn scent, follow this tip. Gather acorns, then drill holes in the center going all the way through. The night before you need to use the acorn scent, soak the acorns overnight in water. The next day, drain the acorns and place them on a paper towel. Microwave the acorns until they sizzle, being careful not to burn them. Use a tongs to transfer the hot acorns to a piece of foil. Wrap the foil around the acorns, and place the bundle in a thermos. When you are ready to release the scent, open the thermos and poke holes in the foil. Replace the thermos lid so it is slightly opened.

Jamie Dowell
Bristol, VA

Here's a tip I picked up a few years ago. I have tested this tip and it really works well.
1. Gather a large amount of fallen acorns.
2. Place acorns in a large pot, and cover with water.
3. Boil until acorns become soft.
4. When acorns are soft, mash with a fork and boil the mixture a little longer.
5. Remove the meat of the acorns and set aside.
6. Pour remaining water into a pump sprayer for a homemade, inexpensive cover scent.
7. Place the mashed pulp from the acorns into film canisters and seal. Use as a scent when you reach your hunting area.

Steve Johnson
Deer Park, TX

THE EXPERT'S NOTEBOOK

Warm Wrists in Cool Weather ... by Jim Shockey

The first thing that gets cold on a late fall hunt is your hands. Take a look at your wrists; what do you see? Veins. Lots of them, right near the surface. Now look where your shirt-sleeve ends, and think about where your gloves or mitts end at the wrist. There's a gap, right? A gap that lets the cold air cool your blood, which of course equals cold hands.

Here's an easy solution. Get an old pair of wool socks; those that have a hole in the toe are perfect for this. Cut off the toe, then pull the sock over your hand and wrist. Note where your thumb wants to stick out, then cut a hole there. Voila! You've just made inexpensive wrist warmers ... and you'll make your hands happy on your next fall trip.

Fool Deer with a Second Stand

If you hunt a specific area for an extended period of time, you may find that the deer eventually figure out you are there. If the deer constantly look up at you, or they seem to be spooked by you when you're in your stand, you may be able to take advantage of that.

Set up a second stand, 15 to 20 yards away from your original stand. Place an extra coat or even a hat in the original treestand, then leave it and move to the second stand. Now, when deer come close, their attention should be focused on the original stand. Hopefully, this will give you a few extra seconds to get a shot in.

Jamie Dowell
Bristol, VA

SPECIAL EXPERT ADVICE

Maps & Patterns

Buy topographical maps and aerial photographs of your hunting areas. Keep detailed notes and marks on these that will help you develop seasonal patterns and species-specific patterns. These patterns, such as sign, sightings, time and weather will be helpful in deciding where and when to begin your hunt, and what species to target. We have been using this system for a number of years, and it has improved our success rate with mule deer, pigs and other game species.

Douglas M. Rodd
Upland, CA

quick tip

Multi-Use Decoys

Here's a tip to help you get more use out of your goose shell decoys.

Get some foam pipe insulation, available from any hardware store. Put it around the base of the shell decoy. You can now use the shells on both land and water. They work best in small, calm water.

Chris Winchester
Cannon Falls, MN

Better Scent Dispersal

quick tip

Carry Special Pen for Big Game Tag

When hunting big game in cold weather, carry a Fisher space pen (available at outdoor gear stores such as REI, Campmor, and Eastern Mountain Sports). These pens write even in sub-zero temperatures and will save you much frustration when filling out your big game tag after a successful hunt.

David Zembiec
Adams, NY

I've been unhappy using the traditional film canisters with cotton for scent dispersal. I've noticed that the cotton becomes wet and gets tightly compacted in the bottom of the film can.

I started using feminine tampons instead (be sure to get unscented ones). I tie a rubber band to the tampon string and loop it over a twig or branch. I hang it two to four feet from the ground, so the scent gets distributed in a 360° radius. I've also found that once I pour the attractant scent on the cotton, it swells to twice its original size. I usually use four to six of these around my stand.

You don't want to leave any sort of non-natural material in the woods after you're done with it, so I also attach a strip of Lewis & Lewis Bright Eye tape around the string. This enables me to easily find my scent dispensers in the evening when I'm leaving my stand. The rubber band is easily cut or pulled off the tree, even in the dark.

Bill Lewis
Egg Harbor, NJ

THE EXPERT'S NOTEBOOK

Ducks: Take Camouflage Seriously ... by Jim Van Norman

The old adage that ducks only see movement when coming into decoys is a mistake. Movement is critical, but ducks of any kind, especially mallards, see far more. Hard-hunted ducks notice changes in vegetation, as well as any odd shape, form or color.

This is especially true when the ducks are familiar with a particular area, such as one they use every day for feeding or resting. Even a subtle change in the surroundings will cause ducks to exhibit considerable concern and avoid your setup.

So camouflage as much as possible. Pick colors that blend with your surroundings. Wear face paint or a face mask, and camo gloves. Make sure the inside of your blind blends with your choice of camo. From a duck's point of view, as it checks out your spread, those dark forms against a light background in that little box down there spells "incoming steel shot!" Blend in completely and your chances of shooting ducks with "gear and flaps down" will improve dramatically.

Extra Warmth from Thermal Underwear

Cut your old thermal underwear off at the knees. Use the scrap material to sew pockets to the thighs. Place Hot Hands in the pockets and wear under your camo and other clothing.

Jamie Dowell
Bristol, VA

SPECIAL EXPERT ADVICE

quick tip

Pack Efficiently

When you are packing your gear for a backpack hunt, remember the following rule: If the item serves the purpose of keeping you alive, then bring it, but if it merely makes you more comfortable, then leave it behind. Remember, whatever gear you plan to bring has to be carried; therefore, weight is critical. Also look at the gear you intend to bring and determine if some items can serve two purposes, eliminating the need for the second item. For instance, a fleecy pair of long johns can also act as a scarf, hat, pillow and in a pinch, a second pair of dry pants to hike in! So why bother carrying these other items? Unless you're some kind of fashion plate, wearing your underwear on your head shouldn't be a big deal, especially when it keeps you from freezing!

Jim Shockey
Duncan, BC

FROM THE EXPERT'S NOTEBOOK

Decoy Repair Tips ... by Chris Winchester

Here are some ways you can repair your plastic or rubber floating decoys.

* The most common problem is decoys with shot holes in them. Before you can repair the holes, you need to drain out any water that has gotten inside the decoy. Drill a hole in the tail near the tip; make sure that your hole is above water level. Drain the water out and allow time for the inside to dry.

* To patch holes, including the hole you may have drilled in the tail to drain water, fill them with silicone or hot glue. Be careful not to get silicone all over the decoy, because it is shiny when dry and may cause birds to flare. Most paints will adhere to silicone, so you can touch up the patched holes once the filler is dry. Another option for patching holes is to melt the plastic back together with a soldering iron, or a metal rod that has been heated up. This works best on very small holes.

* Decoys that are badly cracked or have large leaks can still be salvaged. If they seem to be beyond repair and will never float again, you can cut the bottoms out and use them in a field. They make great confidence decoys for goose hunting. You can also use damaged decoys for decorative purposes. Cut off the keel so the decoy sits well on a table, then use them to decorate the home, cabin, hunting shack, garden or patio.

* Finally, a damaged decoy makes a great piggy bank for a future hunter. Simply cut a slot in the head or back that is about 1/8 inch wide by 1 inch long. You'll have to cut the bottom off when it comes time to get the money out; this is a great incentive for kids to save rather than constantly raiding the piggy bank.

Rattling in Stereo

After one too many times giving myself a rap on the thumb while trying to rattle in a buck, I decided there must be a better way.

I selected a pair of fairly well-matched 8-point racks from my collection in the garage. Then, I attached a 4-inch piece of 1½-inch dowel (closet rod) to the brain side of the skull cap with two 3-inch drywall screws. I then gave the entire setup a coat of hunter orange paint and tied them to each end of a 3-foot length of nylon cord.

I get more realistic sound with these, from tine-tickling to an all-out crash and grind. They are a little harder to carry, but since the skull cap forms a hand guard, I haven't had a black thumbnail for quite a while.

Thomas Galbraith
Cape Coral, FL

quick tip

If you use waterfowl decoys, make a simple "gaff hook" type of tool to help pick them up and to move them around.

Take a very long broomstick or extension pole, then twist a metal hook on the end. This tool will save you lots of time, energy and money. It is also a safe way to pick up decoys that are in the water without the risk of falling in or capsizing the boat.

Matthew Klink
Gaithersburg, MD

FROM THE EXPERT'S NOTEBOOK

Rangefinders: Use Them Early, Put Them Away ... by Jim Van Norman

Rangefinders are great, but many hunters make the mistake of trying to find the range to an animal just before attempting a shot. This extra movement generally causes problems. So do your rangefinding once you are settled in your tree or other stand, memorize the distances and put the rangefinder away. During a stalk, stop short of the place you hope to attempt a shot from, out of sight of the animal, and find the distance to a rock or tree that will be a comparable distance to your quarry. Always do your rangefinding ahead of the moment of truth! Timing is everything, and if you are standing there fumbling with a rangefinder while the critter's getting nervous, you more than likely won't have a good, responsible shot opportunity.

USING A LASER RANGEFINDER

Hunt Smart, Think Like a Deer

For three years, I hunted by sitting on the ground or walking around in the woods. I jumped a deer just once, but by the time I lifted the shotgun up, the deer was out of range. I went home and told my wife that the next year I was going to use a portable treestand and wear good clothing, and then I would get a deer. Well, that's exactly what happened.

Deer are very smart. I think that when deer see too many people walking around in the woods, they change their habits. So we hunters have to learn how to hunt smart and how to think like a deer.

Once I got my treestand, my hunting tactics changed. Now, I

scout to find a nice strong tree for my stand a week before season. I mark the trail to the stand, because I like to be on stand at least an hour and a half before sunrise on opening day.

Before you go out to the woods to hunt, get the right equipment to be out in the cold; otherwise you won't last more than a few hours. Wear clothing made of Gore-Tex, and fleece with Scent-Lok. The Gore-Tex will keep you warm and dry, and the Scent-Lok absorbs your odor, preventing the deer from picking up your scent.

Before I got this new outfit, I used to wear three layers of cotton topped with overalls, and I still couldn't get warm. Cotton is poor insulation for hunting.

All the other hunters I know like to put their deer scent 20 to 30 yards away from their treestand. I do it a little differently. I hang scent bombs a foot above my head. That way, when the wind blows, it carries my scent with the deer scent.

I'd like to tell you the story of a muzzleloader hunt, during which I put together all the new things I've learned. I was in my treestand by 4:35 a.m. Before daylight, I grunted to attract any nearby deer, and at about 6:00 a.m. I saw a little doe come from some thick bushes about 75 yards away. Shortly afterwards, another doe showed up, and this one was big. I let the doe get within about 50 yards and took a shot, but I missed because I failed to calculate the angle when I shot.

After I missed, I realized my shot had been too low. I was so mad and disappointed that I told my buddy I was hanging up my gun and gear. But he told me, "Hey, Henry, don't give up! Everybody misses once in a while." I listened to him and we kept hunting.

On Thanksgiving Day we hunted for a few hours. That day I moved 150 yards down to the valley and set up 20 yards from the thick bushes. After a few hours on stand that morning, I came down from the tree, looked around, and said to myself, "There are no deer around here, but I'm going to attract them."

I grabbed a stick and made a few scrapes on the ground. I sprayed buck and doe urine on top. The next day, we went back to the same spot. As we were walking in, my buddy asked me where I was going to hunt. I told him I was headed for the same tree I'd been in the day before, and that I was going to get my deer from that spot.

At 7:45 a.m., I was still in my stand when I heard all sorts of noise coming from the thick bushes. Suddenly, I saw a nice buck flying through the woods, coming directly at me.

I picked up my gun and thought frantically, trying to come up with a way to get the deer to stop in the opening so I could take a shot. Then I remembered the grunt call I had hanging around my neck.

I grunted twice, freezing the buck at 20 yards away. I fired my muzzleloader, and 75 yards from that spot I found a nice 7-pointer—my first deer in four years. I was jumping, running and doing all kinds of crazy stuff. I could not believe that I had shot a 7-pointer in the mainland. That was two days before the season closed, and I will never forget that Friday. I thought I had been hunting in the past, but *this was the first year I had done it right.*

The moral of my story is this: Invest in the proper equipment and learn how to think like a deer. Dress warm and you'll be able to stay out in the woods until that big buck comes your way!

Henry A. Ledesma
Providence, RI

> *I thought I had been hunting in the past, but this was the first year I had done it right.*

quick tip

Boots for Traction

Mountain hunters may be frustrated when their hard, lugged boot soles slip on snow, wet logs and damp grass. Unless the cleats catch a rock or other edge, the rubber provides little or no traction. A better sole for these conditions is softer rubber with widely spaced nubbins, also known as air-bobs. These wear more quickly than harder Vibram lugs, but stick to more slippery surfaces, an acceptable trade-off when you're trying to follow elk up a mountain.

Even more traction is offered by metal golf cleats. At least one boot maker, Georgia, offers removable cleats in its Ice Trekker line. These offer excellent traction on frozen hillsides and wet logs. Carry various cleat lengths to accommodate varying depths of snow or mud. It may also be possible for a cobbler to re-sole your favorite boots with screw-in cleats.

Ron Spomer
Bloomington, IN

Hunter's Equipment Checklist

CLOTHING

- ❏ Socks
- ❏ Underwear
- ❏ Undershirts (2–4)
- ❏ Long underwear bottoms—synthetic (1–2)
- ❏ Pants—wool or synthetic (2 pair)
- ❏ Shirts—wool or synthetic (2–3 long sleeve)
- ❏ Gloves (2 pair—windblock fleece or wool & a weatherproof shell)
- ❏ Leather gloves (horseback hunters)
- ❏ Hat (1 light & 1 warm)
- ❏ Raingear—tops & bottoms
- ❏ Jacket (1 heavy, 1 light (wear to camp))
- ❏ Vest (down or fleece for cold-weather periods)
- ❏ Handkerchiefs (2–4)
- ❏ Travel clothes (wear to & from camp)

FOOTWEAR

- ❏ Boots (2 pair) w/new laces, well-treated. Rubber hipboots for later moose hunts.
- ❏ Camp shoes (lightweight)
- ❏ Gore-Tex socks
- ❏ Blister kit (moleskin & athletic tape)

SLEEPING

- ❏ Sleeping bag (mummy style)
- ❏ Waterproof stuff sack (or hydroseal sack)
- ❏ Stocking cap or headband
- ❏ Pillow

HUNTING EQUIPMENT

- ❏ Large pack (backpack hunters) w/raincover, 2 nylon straps (3') & extra waist buckle
- ❏ Day pack (horseback/riverboat hunters)
- ❏ Binoculars—waterproof (min. 7 power/30mm obj.)
- ❏ Lens cleaner/cloth
- ❏ 1 compact hunting knife (sharp)
- ❏ 1 compact knife sharpener
- ❏ Hard weapon case (commercial flight)
- ❏ Soft case (for trip on floatplane)

Rifle Hunters

- ❏ Gun & scope (appropriate to species hunted)
- ❏ Scope cover (bikini or flip-up type)
- ❏ 1–2 boxes of shells (premium factory or reloads) & shell holder
- ❏ Compact cleaning rod
- ❏ Cotton patches (1–2 dozen)
- ❏ Bore cleaner
- ❏ Electrical tape
- ❏ Oil or wax & gun grease (rust prevention)

Bowhunters

- ❏ Compound or traditional bow (record brace height, knocking point, axle-axle, etc.)
- ❏ Extra string and/or cables (shot in)
- ❏ Extra rest & sight pins
- ❏ 2 releases (mechanical, tab or glove)
- ❏ Bowsling
- ❏ Armguard
- ❏ Moleskin or adhesive fleece for arrow rest area
- ❏ Arrows (1–2 dozen)
- ❏ Bludgeon, field & judo points (2–3 each)
- ❏ Broadheads (sharp)—1 dozen (3–4 fixed-blades preferred)
- ❏ Quiver
- ❏ Compact/portable bow press
- ❏ Allen wrenches
- ❏ String wax & string silencers

Muzzleloader Hunters

- ❏ Gun (.50 or .54 caliber)
- ❏ Twenty 300-gr. or larger sabot-type slugs
- ❏ Pyrodex pellets or equivalent (90 gr. min. load)
- ❏ Magnum caps
- ❏ Quick loaders (2–3)
- ❏ Breech tool
- ❏ Allen wrench
- ❏ Cleaning rod & jag
- ❏ Bullet puller

Muzzleloader continued ...
- ❑ Breech plug grease/lube
- ❑ Cleaning patches
- ❑ Old toothbrush
- ❑ Cleaning solvent (or use hot water/soap)
- ❑ Waterproof bag/sack
- ❑ Electrical tape

MISCELLANEOUS
- ❑ Camera—compact w/extra batteries & waterproof case (zip-top bag)
- ❑ Film—print (100–400 speed) and/or slide
- ❑ Flashlight/headlamp w/extra batteries & bulb
- ❑ Water bottle
- ❑ Matches in waterproof container & butane lighter
- ❑ Bug repellent (seasonal)
- ❑ Compass w/mirror
- ❑ Sunglasses w/head strap
- ❑ Zip-top bags (4–5 one-gallon size)
- ❑ Garbage bags (2–3, heavy-duty kitchen or larger compactor-type bags best)
- ❑ Pillowcase (2–3 old ones for taking home capes, boned meat & dirty clothes)
- ❑ Book (small paperback)
- ❑ Hunting & fishing license
- ❑ Airline ticket, passport, wallet, credit card & ID
- ❑ Trophy fees (U.S. cash or traveler's checks)

PERSONAL
- ❑ Toothbrush, toothpaste & dental floss
- ❑ Liquid soap (1–2 oz., unscented, for hair & body)
- ❑ Toilet paper (Kleenex pocket packs or TP in a zip-top bag)
- ❑ Lip balm w/SPF 10 minimum
- ❑ Small towel & wash cloth
- ❑ Deodorant (baking soda or no-scent type)
- ❑ Prescription medication (if required)
- ❑ Glasses or contacts (if required)
- ❑ Ibuprofen or aspirin
- ❑ Band•Aids
- ❑ Nail clippers

ADDITIONAL EQUIPMENT
(*Backpack hunters*)
- ❑ Stream crossing shoes (Nike Aqua socks or Glacier socks (if using plastic boots)
- ❑ Sleeping pad (3/4 or full-length)

OPTIONAL
- ❑ Spotting Scope—variable or 30-power fixed
- ❑ Tripod—compact (less than 2 lbs.)
- ❑ Video camera
- ❑ Rangefinder
- ❑ Fishing pole & reel (3 piece or smaller)
- ❑ Gators (Schnee's Gore-Tex fleece—highly recommended)
- ❑ Hipboots
- ❑ Disposable razor
- ❑ Sunblock
- ❑ Bivy sack
- ❑ Flagging tape
- ❑ White painter's suit & black kneepads (goat hunters)
- ❑ Face paint or camo facemask/head net (bowhunters)
- ❑ Safety blanket (lightweight foil type)
- ❑ Extra limbs (bowhunters)
- ❑ Water filter
- ❑ Trekking pole or walking stick (backpack hunters—highly recommended)
- ❑ Baby wipes
- ❑ Athletes' foot/jock itch cream
- ❑ Small notepad & pencil/pen
- ❑ Leather scabbard (horseback hunters)

Bryan Martin
Canadian Mountain Outfitters, Ltd.
Bozeman, MT

Editor's Note
Here's the good news: Use these exhaustive checklists to whittle down to the particulars for your own hunt. Here's the bad news: Now you won't have any more excuses for forgetting essential gear!

Muzzleloader Hunting for Pronghorns

The wind came down from the north, a blast of chilling arctic air blowing over the snowcapped Beaverhead Mountains and out upon the upper Snake River Plain. Eighty miles to the east, the jagged spires of the Tetons were distinctly visible beneath the crimson fire of the sunrise. As the shadows of the departing night gave way to the newborn day, the eyes of the buckskin-clad hunter probed the sagebrush slopes of Cedar Butte for movement. Off in the distance, a band of pronghorns, mere specks of tan and white, moved slowly as they fed. The hunter hefted the battered longrifle he carried, checking his priming, and began to make a stalk to get within shooting range.

What looked like a scene from the early 1800s was in reality a recent hunting trip in eastern Idaho. And the grizzled mountain man attempting to put the sneak on those feeding antelope, well, that was me. Since 1986, I've been fortunate enough to draw out on controlled muzzleloader hunts for pronghorn a number of times and have harvested five of the "prairie goats" thus far. I can truthfully attest that they are a challenge to hunt, perhaps the ultimate for today's blackpowder enthusiast.

When I obtained my first permit, opening day found me on Cedar Butte's broken, sage-covered flanks several miles southwest of Dubois, Idaho. A little preseason scouting had shown me there were good numbers of antelope in the area. I'd started hunting deer with a muzzleloader a few years prior and now I was excited to try it out on these critters. But after a great amount of time spent scuttling about on hands and knees dodging cactus patches and lava rock rubble—once, even a rattlesnake—while attempting to get within blackpowder rifle shooting range of my prey, and then a dozen or so missed shots, I ended the season empty-handed. Not being as familiar with my rifle as I'd thought, and shooting at distances farther than I was used to, proved to be my undoing, coupled with not knowing much of anything about pronghorns or how to hunt them.

LEARNING FROM EXPERIENCE

Another year, I vowed I would be better prepared and my tag would be filled. In fact, the next season that I drew out on the muzzleloader hunt, I was successful in bagging my first antelope! The lessons learned in my initial year made a big difference.

And in the years since, I've continued my education with every hunt I've made. Oh, I'm by far no expert, but perhaps I can pass on a tip or two that can assist you in some way toward making a successful muzzleloader hunt for pronghorns yourself.

Undoubtedly the most difficult aspect in taking an antelope with a blackpowder rifle is getting within shooting range.

THE PRONGHORN CHALLENGE

Undoubtedly the most difficult aspect in taking an antelope with a blackpowder rifle is getting within shooting range. Pronghorn live in wide open spaces, habitat specifically suited to their two main survival mechanisms: their legendary speed and their keen eyesight. As one nineteenth-century hunter swore after unsuccessfully trying to give chase on horseback, "The antelope could outrun a streak of lightning." And their eyesight is nothing less than phenomenal, with an angle of view of some 200 degrees and the ability to detect movement up to four miles away, comparable to looking through 8X binoculars. So getting close, within 100 yards, can be a bit challenging.

EFFECTIVE STRATEGIES

There are a few strategies the blackpowder hunter can employ: stalking, ambushing, decoying and calling.

Stalking

By far the most commonly used method of these is stalking. Because they live in open country, pronghorns aren't hard to spot at long distances. If hunting in broken country, as I found around Cedar

Butte, the hunter has a fair chance of completing a stalk undetected. Using as much of the natural lay of the land as possible to keep out of sight, even if it takes you the long way around, can often put you within range.

If a hunter runs out of good cover to make his stalk, he can usually still get closer by slithering forward on his belly. Antelope don't seem to be as alarmed about a horizontal object as they are about one that is vertical. They probably associate the horizontal form with a four-legged animal, while the upright one would undoubtedly be recognized as a man and danger.

In the case that they do spook during your stalk, it is helpful to know that pronghorns seem to run over two ridges before stopping when alarmed in hilly country like I prefer to hunt in. Seldom will you find them over the first rise, but very often on the other side of the next. So don't despair if the bunch of antelope you are trying to get close to suddenly flash their white rumps your way and race off. It is often possible to follow a fleeing herd and make a new stalk.

When hunting pronghorns, expect to make long stalks and spend a lot of time on your hands and knees. I have made stalks of up to a mile and a half to get within 50 yards of antelope. It ain't easy, but it can be done! The buckskin "mountain man" clothing I choose to hunt in does well to protect me from the many cactus spines and lava rocks I seem to encounter continually while crawling and slithering along. Leather patches on knees and elbows could also prove to be a benefit in making your stalk more comfortable.

Ambushing

Ambushing is basically being where the antelope want to go. Ambushes can be set up at waterholes that the animals are known to be using. But it is important to remember that they don't always water at the same location on a day-to-day basis, nor always at the same time of day. This varies from one area to another, so some preseason scouting can give

Continued …

used. In broken country, pronghorns tend to follow the drainage patterns of the land. The hunter familiar with the daily movements of the antelope in the area he is hunting can often ambush them as they follow their natural travel routes. Once again this is where pre-season scouting pays off.

When hunting from a stand, the hunter must remain as motionless as possible and be totally hidden from view. A blind made from sagebrush or other area vegetation is easy to make and works well. If cover is scanty, a pit can be dug to make a blind. Make sure whatever type of stand you take that you allow yourself enough room to be comfortable over a long period. And above all else, be patient. A shot will present itself if you've chosen a good ambush location. Sometimes it just takes time!

Using Decoys
Decoying is both an old and new concept in antelope hunting. Antelope are wonderfully curious creatures and this trait has proved to be their undoing since mankind first pursued them. Hunters during the days of the mountain men

you an idea of how regularly antelope are coming to a particular waterhole and at what times.

Fence crossings are another good spot to watch for antelope. Pronghorns, though perfectly capable of doing so, will not jump over a fence. Instead, they crawl under where they can, and they will use the same crossings time and time again. Many of these cross points are near fence corners, but they can be found along other stretches depending on the lay of the land and antelope travel routes. A hunter is almost ensured of a shot if he takes up a stand near a regularly-used crossing and is patient.

Preseason scouting can also give you a good idea of how often a particular fence crossing is being employed a method known as "flagging" to lure pronghorn within range of their rifles. To do this, the hunter tied a piece of cloth to the end of his ramrod and waved it above the spot where he was laying in hiding. The inquisitive antelope, upon seeing an unusual object, would approach and thus give the hunter an opportunity for a shot. Similar to this was another ruse used by both the whites and Native Americans of the early 1800s whereby the hunter would lie on his back in the grass and kick his legs in the air. The curious pronghorn would approach to see what the odd sight was, and come within rifle or bow range.

With the blackpowder rifle, the hunter is limited to a single, so before the trigger is pulled he must be absolutely sure of his aim.

In recent years, archery hunters have started using antelope decoys to lure their quarry up close. These seem to be most effective during the mating season in late September, but I've found them to work at other times of the year as well. On occasion, I've used a decoy to bring antelope closer to my blind, though I would not recommend this if there is the possibility that modern high-powered rifles are being used in your hunting area. Because of the limited range of blackpowder weapons, I feel relatively safe using my decoy under the right conditions. However, I don't hide behind it as archery hunters sometimes do, but rather at a distance off to the side.

Calling

Another proven way to lure pronghorn antelope into range is with a call. They will come on the run sometimes, or other times will walk stiff-legged to the sound of a high-pitched predator call designed for fox or coyote. Perhaps they believe it is the bleat of a young antelope, or it may just be another manifestation of their overwhelming curiosity. I have also heard that making calf sounds with a cow elk call will work to entice them to come near. I've seen antelope calls on the market, but I've yet to actually try one to see how they work (though I've got a feeling they probably do as well as the other calls I am familiar with).

MORE KEYS TO SUCCESS

Although getting within shooting range is the most challenging part of the hunt, other factors come into play that help determine whether the hunter is successful or not.

Judging Distance

One of the most important factors, and one that foiled me a number of times during my earlier hunts, is correctly estimating yardage. In open country, animals often appear to be closer than they really are. It's important to spend as much time as possible under conditions similar to those you'll experience in the area you plan to hunt. With the blackpowder rifle, the hunter is limited to a single, so before the trigger is pulled he must be absolutely sure of his aim. Not many pronghorns will stand around long enough to let you reload once they've been shot at.

Selecting Equipment

The pronghorn hunter should be prepared to make shots out to 100 yards and farther. For such long-range shooting the .50 caliber rifle should be considered the minimum effective bore size. A barrel 34- to 40-inches long, offering a longer sight radius for more positive sighting, is also preferable. I would recommend using a maximum powder charge (110 grains for .50 caliber, 120 grains for .54 caliber) when using a patched round ball as I do for hunting. Plus, when you take into consideration that there is always a breeze blowing in antelope country, well, it makes each of these recommendations even more important to keep your bullet on the mark when you shoot.

Continued …

Using a Rest

It is a good idea to use a rest when shooting at game at such long ranges as the antelope hunter does. If available, a tree or a rock will do nicely, but because of the nature of most antelope country, these aren't often found. Many of the old-timers used a set of "cross sticks," simply two crossed sticks attached at the center. When spread apart, they formed an X-shaped rest that the forearm of the rifle could be steadied on. Others simply used their ramrod as a rest, one end of it stuck in the ground. A walking stick or staff would also serve the same purpose if the hunter had such along. But no matter what kind of rest is used, the fact remains that the steadier the hold, the more accurate the shot will be.

Placing the Shot

Accuracy is especially important when shooting at an animal the size of the pronghorn with a limited vital zone. A unique physical characteristic of the antelope, though, is that its vital area is convenient-ly marked for the hunter. The white markings of its belly and side meet with the tan "saddle" in a line just above the elbow, marking the vertical line of the crosshairs at the vital spot. A ball placed here by the marksman will without a doubt score a lethal hit.

ENJOYING THE CHALLENGE

In the years since my first pronghorn hunt, I have ventured onto the sagebrush plains of Idaho armed not only with that well-worn longrifle of mine, but also with a wealth of pronghorn hunting lore I learned mostly the hard way. And in the majority of those years, I have returned home in triumph. The pronghorn antelope is, as I see it, the ultimate challenge for the muzzleloading hunter, but by combining the ingredients of stealth, planning and patience, even the novice can be successful.

Terry D. Baddley
Boise, ID

THE EXPERT'S NOTEBOOK

Waterfowl Hunting Tips ...
by Chris Winchester

—When you're picking up decoys from the water in cold weather, wear a simple pair of inexpensive jersey gloves. Your hands will still get wet, but the gloves will help keep them warm by protecting them from the wind.

—After removing a boat from the water in cold weather, be sure to put the outboard all the way down and start it for ten seconds. This will help remove all the water and keep it from freezing in the gearcase.

—When you're hunting in the snow, or when you're hunting snow geese, just purchase a white fleece sweatsuit rather than a full, expensive suit of the special snow camo. The white fleece sweatsuit also works well for predator hunting.

—If you hunt a lot of deep water but occasionally also hunt small shallow ponds, glue a spring-type clothespin under each of your decoys to clip the decoy cord into. This way, you won't have so much excess cord in the water.

quick tip

ATVs: Cushion Your Equipment

To prevent jarring equipment when using an ATV, place an egg crate between the rack and equipment.

Jamie Dowell
Bristol, VA

THE EXPERT'S NOTEBOOK

Muffs vs. Mitts ... by Jim Shockey

In bitter cold weather, forget wearing bulky mitts and instead wear a thin pair of gloves and a muff. No matter how fancy a mitt is, with an extra shooting finger stitched in, or a slit to slide your finger out, it isn't as practical for shooting as a muff. I'd be willing to bet that pulling off a mitt is a good second slower than pulling your hands from a muff. And in terms of whitetail hunting, where two seconds is how long you have to make the average shot, one second is the difference between success and failure! I wear my muff around my neck on a string, not only so I can't lose it but so it doesn't drop to the ground when I pull my hands out. Mitts have to be removed and have to be placed somewhere. That's extra movement that you don't need.

quick tip

Follow Up a Blood Trail

Here's a tip that can work for any big game. I've always used it for bear; because of their thick, matted fur, they sometimes don't leave a very good blood trail to follow.

Fill a small spray bottle with peroxide (about eight ounces is all you'll need), and add a few drops of yellow food coloring. Keep this bottle in your pack. If you lose a blood trail, start at your last sign and spray the grass, leaves and bushes. The peroxide will foam up when it's sprayed on even the smallest drop of blood, and from my experience, yellow food coloring helps it show up the best.

Robert A. Torti III
Thompson Falls, MT

Different Uses for Common Items

Here are a few tips I can give about using things in ways you might not have thought about.

Opening day of the Wisconsin rifle deer season found me on stand at 5:30 a.m., an hour before daylight. I heard deer walking past me in the dark, headed for their bedding areas. When daylight finally did arrive, there were no deer in sight.

By 8:45 a.m., I still had seen no deer and was getting pretty bored, so I took out my slingshot and some ¾-inch ball bearings I had brought. I hurled a ball bearing about 80 yards so it landed near a beaver dam by a bedding area. I picked up my rifle and started scanning the area. To my surprise, out came a nice 10-pointer. Without that slingshot, the buck wouldn't have come out.

My second tip will come in handy for those who practice shooting but don't have a solid shooting rest. Try using an old ironing board. It is convenient to have a small chair to sit on also. The ironing board is adjustable to any height you need, plus it folds away neatly for storage and doesn't weigh much.

Randy Leibl
Arpin, WI

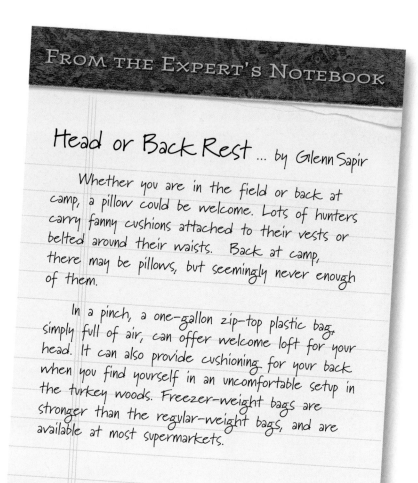

FROM THE EXPERT'S NOTEBOOK

Head or Back Rest ... by Glenn Sapir

Whether you are in the field or back at camp, a pillow could be welcome. Lots of hunters carry fanny cushions attached to their vests or belted around their waists. Back at camp, there may be pillows, but seemingly never enough of them.

In a pinch, a one-gallon zip-top plastic bag, simply full of air, can offer welcome loft for your head. It can also provide cushioning for your back when you find yourself in an uncomfortable setup in the turkey woods. Freezer-weight bags are stronger than the regular-weight bags, and are available at most supermarkets.

Crunch Time

I like crunch time. It's that last half-hour or so of shooting light on a crisp fall evening when the woods go quiet. Squirrels go to bed. Partridge and turkeys go to roost. That's when you hear the crunch … the four-footed crunch of a deer working its way toward your tree-stand. This is why you sit for the last three hours—to relish the last few minutes of crunch time.

Sweating the details might give me a little edge, and can turn hope into confidence.

Just such an evening found me high on a ridge a few years ago. The acorns were falling heavily on the little flat of oaks just below a thick spruce knob. There I was, perched in a little maple, my stand turned in to a small spruce growing beside it. It was a choice setup. A small cliff ran down one side of the shelf. It was just enough to funnel the deer to these oaks as they left their beds up in the spruces.

A decent rub line started near my stand, and I'd sweetened the deal by making a hooking of my own next to a real rub with a de-scented wood rasp I keep handy. I try to keep everything de-scented: me, my clothes, my boots, backpack, tree steps and stand. No sweaty old watch bands, wallets and such. I've been told that I'm crazy to do all the rituals I perform. Yeah, right—crazy like a fox. Sweating the details might give me a little edge, and can turn hope into confidence.

Back to me in that maple. I'd slid in there, put on rubber gloves, hung the stand, snipped two small shooting lanes and never raised a sweat. This is the pop-tart method. Pop in, toast 'em, and pop out. The best kind of deer to hunt is the kind that doesn't know it's being hunted.

And it was that kind of deer that I could hear, working its way toward my ambush at crunch time. As I eyeball the wind thread hanging from my bow limb, my ears attend to the footsteps coming closer. I can see the buck now: a tolerable buck, maybe six or eight points. It's coming from behind and to my right and is about to hit my entry trails. It seems concerned with nothing. Apparently the scrubbing I gave my rubber boots before I left home was worth the effort.

The buck is now approaching my shooting lane to my right, and I slowly get ready. However, an oak behind me drops a few acorns, and the buck turns to head for them. Now it's coming around to my left, when suddenly its head comes up. I'm busted! But no, the buck is looking below and past me to the mock rub I made. It starts walking toward the rub. I'm ready, but I won't take a frontal shot. Luckily, a small blowdown is in the buck's way, forcing it to turn. The string tracker on my arrow is like a tracer in the fading light. It won't be needed, though, as the arrow strikes the deer in the spine and knocks it off its feet. A second arrow

is quickly sent, and the woods grow silent but for the pounding of my heart.

I remove my head net and lower my accoutrements to the ground. I walk 13 paces to the buck. The feelings I have as I look at this enchanted creature are hard to describe. For me, hunting is a paradox. To fulfill the hunt, I must kill that which I love and admire. There is no catch-and-release hunting, and I wouldn't want there to be. But there's always a touch of sadness that mingles with the elation of a successful hunt. A much wiser bowhunter than I once said: "When the hunter is in a treestand with high moral values and with the proper hunting ethics and richer for the experience, that hunter is 20 feet closer to God." I think he said it all. Good hunting, and shoot straight.

Bill Torrey
Jericho, VT

Warm Up Your Scent

Warm scent disperses better than cold scent. Here's a way to warm up your deer scent.

Fill a thermos with boiling water. Place a piece of plastic cling wrap over the top, and press gently in the center to create an indentation. Secure the edges of the plastic wrap with a rubber band wrapped below the threads of the thermos, then replace the lid.

When you get to your hunting spot, open the lid of the thermos and pour some scent into the indentation. The scent will be warmed by the hot water, and will disperse easily. The water stays hot for a long time, too.

Jamie Dowell
Bristol, VA

FROM THE EXPERT'S NOTEBOOK

Small Binoculars, Big Scope ... by Jim Shockey

If carrying full-sized binoculars gives you a pain in the neck, consider combining mini-binocs with a full-sized spotting scope, especially if you're trophy hunting for open country species such as mule deer, pronghorn and sheep. In my experience, tiny binoculars are more than adequate for locating game. Once an animal is spotted, even the best full-size glass of 7X to 10X power is of limited value for determining trophy potential. That's when you need to switch to a 20X to 45X spotting scope. So why carry heavy binoculars? In recent years, I've been using either a pair of 10X28 Leupold (11 ounces) or 10X25B Zeiss (8 ounces) roof prism binoculars backed by a 20-60X 77mm Bausch & Lomb (Bushnell) Elite spotting scope. The big scope weighs 3 pounds, but with its bright, color-corrected image I can count antler tines often more than a mile away, and this saves lots of time and energy. Many times I've spotted bucks and bulls before my guides did with their full-sized binoculars. This system makes more sense than using heavyweight binocs and trying to sneak by with a diminutive, dim spotting scope that can't resolve a sharp image at 1,000 yards.

JIM SHOCKEY

The Well-Equipped Turkey Vest

I've been an NAHC Life Member for some time. A few years ago, I purchased a turkey hunting vest through the Club. It has lots of room for "stuff," it's comfortable to wear, and it allows for hands-free movement to and from my hunting spot. Here is what I carry in my vest:

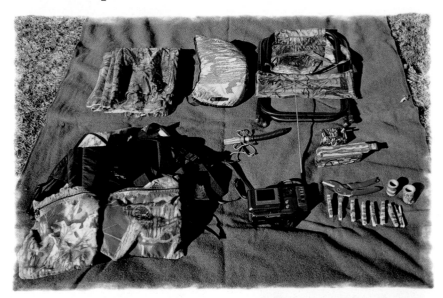

- 20- X 4-foot camo netting for blind
- Aluminum folding chair
- Spring clothespins
- Camo tape
- Brush snippers
- Wool blanket (if needed for a really cold sit)
- Grunt tube and turkey calls
- "Bun saver" (blow-up pillow)
- Compact VHS camcorder, batteries, TV adapter

I know what you're probably thinking: "Why all that stuff?" Well, I was run over by a gravel truck when I was five years old, so my back isn't real good now. I need the support of the chair back. The blind enables me to move the lower half of my body a little now and then, without being too obvious. The clothespins, which I cover with the camo tape, allow me to hang up my net almost anywhere. Snippers, blanket and game calls are self-explanatory.

The inflatable cushion can help relieve physical discomfort in more ways than one. Of course, it makes a softer cushion for your behind, but I find that it also helps to periodically let some of the air out of the cushion, which puts your body in a slightly different position, which helps you feel like a new person when you think you just can't sit still for another minute. Regular foam cushions don't allow "adjusting" like this.

In order to sit still, you need to keep your mind active. I enjoy watching squirrels, grouse, woodpeckers and blue jays, but you can do that only so long before getting restless. A few years ago, I convinced my wife that I needed a new video camera. The one I have has a small screen and an ear phone cord, and takes color images. I've allowed this to entertain me for many hours while in a blind or on my treestand. And when most hunters are at home watching the game on TV, I can watch the woods.

Vernon Denzer
Dane, WI

These pictures show the vest before and after it is packed. There is still room for a sandwich, apple, thermos and more.

FROM THE EXPERT'S NOTEBOOK

Add Motion to Your Decoys ... by Chris Winchester

Attach one end of a 100-yard-long decoy string to the bottom of a floating decoy. Run the string through the hole in a brick and drop the brick near the decoy, keeping hold of the string as the brick drops. Place a second brick on shore near your blind; run the string through the second brick and then into your blind. When birds are coming in, pull the string and the decoy will move. This trick works especially well in small ponds and potholes.

Field Gear that Works

Here are some tips about various types of field gear that I've used for years. Small things like this really add up to a big advantage when you're out hunting.

- For years, my son and I have been using hydration systems while hiking and backpacking, and they work just as well for hunting. We've found it better to sip water frequently via a tube and bite valve than to guzzle water at irregular intervals. This really helps maintain performance during outdoor activities. We use the Gregory Mirage System (Gregory Mountain Products, 800-477-3420). The taste-free bladder holds up to 110 ounces of water and can be installed in a variety of backpacks and fanny packs. During very cold weather, it pays to blow the water from the tube back into the bag, and cover the unit with a jacket while you sleep, to eliminate ice problems in the tube and valve. I simply don't travel in the mountains without this extremely useful piece of equipment.

- Anyone who backpacks or sleeps on the ground knows the benefits of a sleeping pad. These lightweight pads insulate you from heat loss due to conductivity with the cold ground. But they are useful for more than just sleeping. How often have you found yourself hunting on a cold day, with your keister resting on a cold rock or stand? Your rear end is funneling the body heat right out of you. Simply get some half-inch-thick Ensolite or

Evasote, and cut it to match the shape of the back of your day pack. Place it in the pack, against your back. While you're traveling it will keep other items from poking your back, and when you need a ground pad, just pull it out and sit on it. These products are made from closed-cell foam, so they are not only lightweight but they repel moisture. You'll be warm, comfortable and dry.

- Next time you're hiking to your favorite stand during the dark of night, trying to start your generator or doing anything else that requires you to have a light in the dark, try a head lamp. It's the hands-free, efficient way to accomplish your task.

- The "less is more" concept applies to almost everything you do, at least in the mountains. I learned this concept from backpacking and mountain climbing, and have applied it to hunting with great success. Through tips like the ones here, as well as your own experience, you'll learn to recognize essential gear and how much of it you really need. This applies to everything: how much and what type of clothing, how to layer, how many bullets, how much trail mix or water, size of your day pack, etc.

Layne T. Oliver
West Valley, UT

quick tip

Socks for Stalking

Stalking close to an animal requires patience and some talent. But this tip will improve your odds, even if you possess little of either.

Noise blows many a stalk. Usually, your boot crunches something and your game takes a hike. That's why I carry a pair of extra-heavy knee-high grey wool socks. When I need to get through a noisy-looking area, out come my wool socks. I take off my boots and pull the wool socks over my other socks, over my knees on the outside of my pants (pant cuffs may swish on vegetation, and the wool eliminates that problem).

Wool is a very quiet fabric. You feel everything underfoot, and can avoid crunching any noise-makers inadvertently. Save this tactic for the last hundred yards of your stalk, to minimize the number of cactus spires, sand burrs and other "stickers" you have to pull out later.

Jim Van Norman
Edgerton, WY

quick tip

Rake a Path to Your Stand

Have you ever stumbled to your deer stand, crunching leaves, brushing against branches, using your flashlight when you really didn't want to shine light in the woods, and still wandered around aimlessly, spreading scent and wasting time trying to find your designated location?

Rake a path to your treestand. Using a heavy-duty rake—molded plastic ones are very durable—clear a yard-wide path from your starting point, or easy-to-find midway mark, directly to your stand. You'll be surprised how easy the task is. The results will pay off with an easy-to-follow, quiet-to-walk path into and out of the woods, even in the dark. You may not even need a flashlight.

An extra bonus, as tracks will reveal, is that deer will often adopt the quiet path you have created!

Glenn Sapir
Shrub Oak, NY

"Scent Line" Brings Buck In

When using scents, don't be afraid to try something different. One of my hunting buddies, Allen Plumline, had seen a buck with a nice rack entering a cut cornfield about 300 yards from one of my stands one evening. Using this information the next afternoon, I took a four-foot stick and tied two three-foot-long cords and drag rags to the stick. I then went to where Allen said the buck entered the field the evening before and started my scent line.

I used Doe-in-Heat on one scent rag and tarsal gland scent on the other rag. This was to simulate a buck trailing a "hot doe." I dragged the scent rags about 300 yards to my stand, freshening the scent rags about every 75 yards to keep the scent strong. When I was done I put the stick with the scent rags in a low bush about eight yards from my stand.

About two hours later as I was on stand with my bow, I saw the buck emerge from the opposite side of the woodline about 350 yards away. The buck started to feed in the field and luckily angled toward my scent line. When the deer smelled the scent line he began to follow it. At about 50 yards out, the buck made a 90-degree turn in the field where I had turned while walking to my stand, and I knew the buck would come all the way into my setup.

The big-bodied buck walked in like he was on a string and started sniffing the rags in the

bush. The 140-pound 9-pointer was mine with a well-placed double lung shot from eight yards. Without the scent line, I never would have gotten the buck to come into my area for a shot.

One note: When making a scent line don't drag the scent directly to the base of your tree or blind. You don't want the deer coming directly at you. You want the buck to come in off to the upwind side of your ambush location. Finally, scent lines and scent posts will not work every time, but don't give up because when they do work, the results can be awesome.

William D. Trout Jr.
Bridgeton, NJ

FROM THE EXPERT'S NOTEBOOK

Stand Approach Scent Control...
by Chuck Adams

Some bowhunters ignore scent management when going to, or sitting in, a treestand or ground blind. Deer that pass by will often detect this mistake and vanish like smoke.

Before heading to your stand, spray your entire lower body with a scent-purging agent like Scent Shield to remove human odor from the surface. Even if you touch occasional foliage as you walk, you won't leave enough deer-scaring odor behind to cause hunting problems.

Wear all-rubber calf-high or hip boots to and from your stand, and complete your scent barrier precautions with commercial scent-blocker pants and jacket. The activated charcoal in such garments soaks up human scent like a sponge.

Always approach your stand on the downwind side, and follow a pre-planned route through the lowest, thinnest foliage around. Careful bowhunters often prune paths to their stands to avoid touching brush, limbs and high grass, all of which can hold human scent for hours.

quick tip

Anchor Your Head Net

If you wear a camo head net during bow season, you've probably had the same experience I have: when you draw to anchor, the net moves over your eye, blowing your shot.

Here's a solution I've been using for a number of years. Get an old pair of glasses with a sturdy frame (or buy cheap reading glasses), then pop out the lenses. Turn your camo net inside out, and sew the eye piece to the net. Turn the net right-side out again. You can now put on your head net just like glasses; the net won't move.

Michael J. Amberman
South Hamilton, MA

Sharp Shooting

There are many archery hunters who miss shots at deer every season simply because they don't spend enough time practicing and fine-tuning their bow. Every bowhunter is going to miss a shot sooner or later; this is something that just happens once in a while, even to the best hunters. But I believe that most hunters miss shots on live animals simply because they lack confidence in their abilities and/or their equipment.

The only way you can become a great shot with your bow is to practice before, during and even after the hunting season ends. This means shooting year-round. That doesn't mean you have to get out in the heat of summer and shoot 40 or 50 arrows. Simply go out a couple days each week and shoot eight or ten arrows each time. This helps you stay familiar with your bow, and also helps keep your shooting muscles in shape.

A bowhunter can also greatly improve his or her skills by practicing on lifelike 3-D targets. I feel these are a must for the serious bowhunter. Three or four targets placed in different areas and different positions will help the hunter become more familiar with distance and point of impact. A hunter needs to know *where* to place the arrow in a deer, whether the animal is quartering away from or toward the

hunter's position. Anyone who has bowhunted long enough knows that perfect, unobstructed broadside shots are rare in the big deer woods. So place your targets behind small trees and brush so you can practice pinpointing the vital area.

Deer just never seem to stop when we want them to. So being a good shot using these practice methods could mean the difference between filling your tag and going home empty-handed.

If you hunt from a treestand, make sure you practice from your stand using these methods, because the angle of your arrow will be different than if you were standing on the ground. Be sure to also practice a straight-down shot from the stand. You may be surprised at how quickly a deer can be right below you. It's always better to let the deer get a little distance away from you for a better shot, but that isn't always possible. Knowing the impact point on a deer that is right below you is very important. As bowhunters, we owe it to our sport to become the best shot that we can, but most of all, we owe it to the deer we hunt.

Pete McCloud
Ironton, OH

Knowing the impact point on a deer when shooting from a tree-stand is very important. If you were to hold right behind the shoulder (as you would from the ground), the arrow would exit out the bottom of the deer, missing the vital areas (Figure A).

Aiming a little higher lets you penetrate down through the vital areas (Figure B).

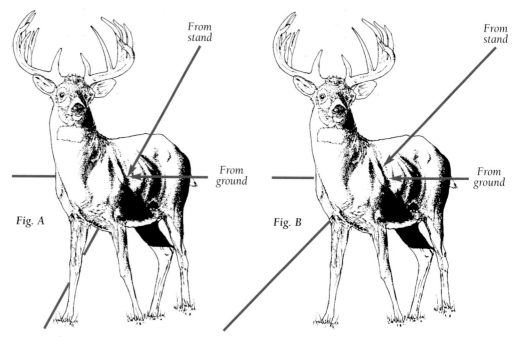

Fig. A   From stand   From ground

Fig. B   From stand   From ground

Two Views on Shooting Sticks

Many hunters know how valuable shooting sticks can be for a steady shot. But shooting sticks should not be left in their holster until it's time for a shot. They make just as much sense for steadying binoculars for a clear view since glassing takes up far more time than shooting. Besides, you can't shoot what you don't see!

Douglas M. Rodd
Upland, CA

If you like having support while shooting a rifle or handgun but you're out in the woods without any equipment, simply make your own shooting sticks. Find two long sturdy sticks, then force them into the ground. Rest your firearm in the notch formed by the "V" of the sticks, and you will have a better, steadier shot.

Lorenzo Arroyo
Llano, TX

quick tip

Fake Bear Marks

If you hunt bears, take a "garden claw" and use it to make scrapes on tree bark in your hunting area (make sure it is okay to do this in your region first). The marks may fool a bear into thinking another bear is in its territory.

A similar tactic works for deer and other scrape-making animals. Use real or artificial antlers, or that garden claw, to make scrapes in your hunting zone. Freshen up your scrapes with one or two different urine scents from the species you're hunting. Make sure there is a good licking branch above the "scrape." To make it look even more realistic, make hoof prints around the area.

Matthew Klink
Gaithersburg, MD

THE EXPERT'S NOTEBOOK
Dry Towels For Better Vision
... by Ron Spomer

If you use glass to assist in seeing game, you need quick access to a drying towel. Whether eyeglasses, binoculars, spotting scope or rifle scope, if it's glass in the hunting fields, chances are it'll get steamed, fogged, sweated, rained on or snow-covered just when you need a clear view. Be ready to clean your glass at all times by carrying several dry, absorbent handkerchiefs, dish cloths or similar quick wipes in an easily accessible pocket. Usually an outer breast pocket is best. To make sure I have such mop-up rags when and where I need them, I stick a small one in each of my shirt breast pockets and any external jacket breast pockets. In addition, I put one inside a zip-top bag in a jacket or pant pocket and another in my pack. When one gets too damp to function properly, I relegate it to a pant cargo pocket and move a fresh one to the most accessible breast pocket. That way I'm ready to wipe off glasses or scope as necessary when a quick shooting opportunity arises.

THE EXPERT'S NOTEBOOK

Pop-Up Magnum Goose Decoy Chair ...
by Chris Winchester

This is an inexpensive field chair for goose hunters. It consists of a wooden platform with a backrest where the hunter will lie. A magnum goose decoy, with slots for visibility, covers the hunter and wood. When geese are in shooting range, the hunter quickly unhooks a wire and the decoy springs back, uncovering the hunter completely.

You will be able to make four of these from a single sheet of plywood. The materials list at right and instructions that follow show you how.

MATERIALS LIST

1 – 12" X 48" piece of ¾-inch plywood
2 – 12-inch-long heavy-duty piano hinges
   ½-inch wood screws (one for each hole in the 2 piano hinges plus 2 additional)
1 – 12-inch length of 1-inch slat
15 – 1½-inch wood screws
1 – 12-inch length of 1" X 6" lumber
1 – 12-inch length of 2" X 2" lumber
1 – Super Magnum Flambeau decoy
1 – 24-inch length of picture hanging wire
1 – Bungee cord

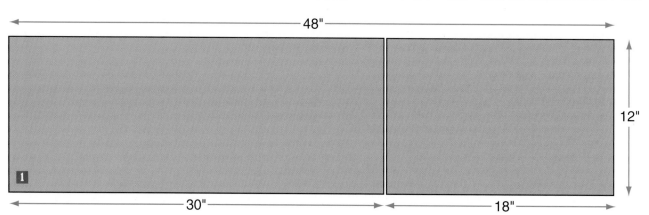

1. Cut the plywood into two sections—one that is 30 inches wide and the other, 18 inches wide.

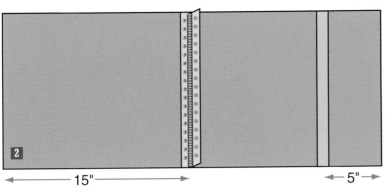

← 15" → ← 5" → ← 8" →

2. Use ½-inch wood screws to attach the left side of a piano hinge at the midpoint of the 30-inch piece as shown. Use six 1½-inch screws to attach the 1-inch slat 5 inches from the right edge as shown. This piece will be the base.

3. Make the backrest: Attach the left side of the other piano hinge 8 inches from the left edge of the 18-inch piece, using ½-inch wood screws.

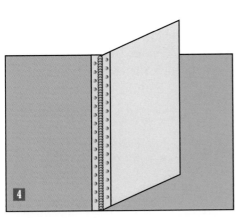 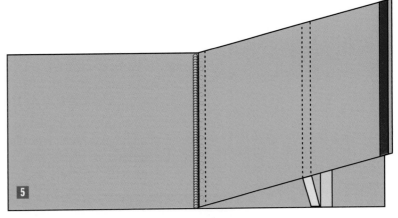

4. To complete the backrest, fasten the right side of the piano hinge to the 1" X 6" as shown, using ½-inch wood screws.

5. Turn the backrest over, so the 1" X 6" side is facing down. Rotate the base piece so the hinge folds to the right, then fasten the backrest to the free side of the piano hinge as shown, using ½-inch wood screws. When properly assembled, the piano hinge will be on the inside angle between the base and the backrest; the 1" X 6" piece will drop down and wedge against the 1-inch slat, positioning the backrest at a comfortable angle. Use six 1½-inch screws to fasten the 2" X 2" (shown in dark brown for clarity) to the head of the backrest; attach the screws through the back side of the backrest so the screw heads are underneath.

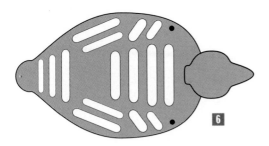

6. LEFT: Cut viewing slots in the decoy (shown from the top); experiment to find the positions that work best for you. Drill a ⅛-inch hole on each side of the decoy, about a quarter of the way back and an inch up from the bottom edge. Attach a screw to the tail of the decoy on the inside.

7. RIGHT: Attach the decoy to the backrest by driving two 1½-inch screws through the drilled holes in the decoy and into the 2" X 2"-inch piece. Screw the picture-hanging wire to the front of the base.

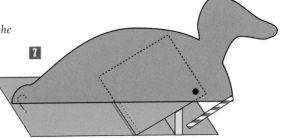

To use, fasten the bungee cord to the back of the base and to the front of the decoy; you'll have to experiment to find the length of bungee cord that produces the right amount of spring. Hook the wire around the screw in the tail of the decoy. When ready to shoot, unhook the wire and the decoy will spring open.

Hot Scent

Warm scent disperses into the air better than cold scent. Here's the way I warm up my deer attractor scent and keep it warm. I prefer a "doe in estrus" scent for this method, but you can use whatever scent you like.

Activate a small chemical hand warmer, such as Hot Hands. Tape it around the outside of a 35mm film canister. Place the wrapped canister into a plastic zip-top bag, leaving about one-quarter inch of the canister sticking out of the bag. Tape the bag where it meets the canister, to keep the canister in place. Now tape the entire unit to a tree that is 30 to 70 yards from your stand; make sure the canister remains upright. Fill the canister with scent, and wait for the action!

Jamie Dowell
Bristol, VA

quick tip

Inexpensive Apple Scent

For those of you who hunt near an apple orchard, or who like to use apple scent for a cover or attractant scent, you can save yourself some money by using apple cider from the grocery store instead of the apple-type deer lure sold in sporting goods stores. A one-ounce bottle of apple lure usually costs $4 to $5, while a gallon of apple cider is only about $4 in most areas. The apple cider has a sweet aroma that can draw deer from long distances.

Will Trout
Bridgeton, NJ

Selecting & Preparing Antlers for Rattling

- Instead of choosing a matched set of antlers, try using different-sized antlers. The tone produced by antlers varies depending on the mass and size. A mismatched set puts out different tones to better simulate two different-sized bucks fighting.

- Before using natural antlers for rattling, cut off the eye guards. This is for safety reasons; it will keep you from goring yourself.

- Cut a quarter-inch off the remaining points and round them with a file. This helps prevent antler chips from flying off during your rattling, possibly hitting you in the face and eyes.

- Secure your horns together with a piece of leather or nylon cord, leaving about 20 inches between them. This keeps the antlers together, making it easier to carry them.

- Finally, here's a piece of advice, based on my own experience. If you're out there rattling and you start to feel you've been waiting too long and nothing is going to show up, wait longer. The deer I bagged in the 1999 season took 3½ hours to rattle in.

Robert A. Torti III
Thompson Falls, MT

FROM THE EXPERT'S NOTEBOOK

Two Tips for Keeping Dry

Next time you find yourself forced to cross deep creeks without hip boots, try speed and raingear to keep your feet dry. Gore-Tex boots and pants work best for this, but even wool pants will do. The trick is to lace the tops of boots tightly and splash across the stream as quickly as possible. By the time the pant legs soak up their fill of water, you should be across with dry feet. An even drier approach is to tie the cuff around the boot top/ankle with a lace, duct tape or even long grass stems twisted together.

If you're wearing Gore-Tex or other waterproof pants, you're almost home free. Tape these around your waterproof boot tops and you can almost leisurely cross knee-deep streams. The key is a tight seal.
—Ron Spomer

You can spend a lot of money on expensive foul-weather gear, and the space-age construction can certainly help keep you dry and warm. But if you'd rather not wear or tote that type of extra clothing, throw a heavy-duty garbage bag into your hunting vest or backpack. Simply cut holes for your head and arms, and you have a fairly effective poncho. The common dark-green bags offer suitable camouflage, and the clear bags will expose your camo or hunter-orange outerwear. If you search hard enough, perhaps in a hardware or home supply store rather than the supermarket, you may even find hunter-orange garbage bags.
—Glenn Sapir

Make Your Own Hunting Tips Book

After years of saving hunting magazines (including *North American Hunter*), I just plain ran out of room. Instead of trashing the whole lot, I went through each one of them, cut out the most interesting articles and put them in plastic sleeves. The sleeves went into a binder, which is now my ultimate hunting reference guide, full of years of information that pertains to my interests. This is also a good way to keep track of various trends in hunting methods and equipment.

Randy Lambert
Simcoe, ONT

FROM THE EXPERT'S NOTEBOOK

A Little Bull Is Good for Elk ... by Jim Van Norman

When hunting elk, use a call that portrays a small, young bull. Not even the biggest bull elk wants to fight the meanest, toughest bull on the mountain. So portray a "cocky youngster" who is too big for his britches.

Once a bull has answered and you get his basic position, challenge back and forth a couple times to determine if he might come to you. Generally, he won't. Then it's time to put the pressure on him. Pinpoint his position and go to him. Get in as close as you dare, get set up and switch to a cow-in-heat call. The bull will likely bugle back at your cow call. Then, with all your might, give him some more "cocky" young bull sass. But be ready, because things are going to start popping! Use this combination in the woods and you will get more action—from bulls of all sizes—than with any other tactic.

Use a Rope for Rattling

I am an NAHC Life Member and have been rattling deer to my bow and gun stands for more than 31 years. My rattling technique is different from most. All you need to try it is something you probably already have with you: a long rope.

My stand is usually 20 feet up, and I always use a quarter-inch nylon rope to pull my bow or gun up once I'm in my stand. The rope is long enough that one end can lie on the ground when the other end is in the stand with me. After I pull up my gun or bow, I tie my rattling antlers to the rope and lower them to the ground, then tie the other end to my treestand.

When I want to rattle, I simply use one hand to lift the antlers from the ground and give them a few quick jerks. This allows the antlers to click gently together. I also lift the antlers and then let them drop to the ground, to imitate the sound of a deer's hooves on the forest floor.

I've often found that this is all that is needed to get a buck to move in close enough for a shot. This method also allows me to hold my gun or bow in one hand, while using the other hand to jerk and drop the antlers. I think this is an improvement over the traditional rattling method, which requires the use of both hands and also causes extra movement that might be caught by that wise buck.

During a recent season, while hunting from my treestand along the Scioto River in Marion County, Ohio, I shot the buck of a lifetime. At about 8:00 a.m., I saw the buck walking on the far bank of the river, 100 yards away. As I began jerking and dropping my antlers, the buck trotted up along the river, crossed at a low spot and headed for my stand.

The buck held up twice, and each time, I jerked the antlers slightly and blew softly on my doe bleat call. When the buck was about 35 yards away, I placed a sabot slug behind its shoulder with my Remington 11-87. Fifteen minutes later, I was looking at the largest buck I'd ever seen in the wild. It had 15 scorable points, with a 22-inch spread. The gross score was 170 inches, and the buck weighed 227 pounds. I am certain that my rattling technique helped me pull the buck across the river and into shotgun range.

Sam Derugen
Woodward, PA

photography • camp tips • firestarting • weather & wind

OUTDOOR OBSERVATIONS

Good hunters are in tune with weather and other natural phenomena, not only by necessity but by choice. In this chapter, you'll benefit from the experiences of fellow NAHC Members as they share tips for outdoor skills ranging from keeping dry in the field, to knot-tying and other camp necessities, to photography tips that will help you preserve a record of your hunt.

Treestand Safety

One fall afternoon, after putting in a hard day at work, I was looking forward to sitting in my treestand for a few hours to relax and maybe shoot a deer. I had been hunting almost every day since opening day, but was waiting for a bigger deer.

After driving home from work, I changed into my hunting clothes, put my bow in my truck and headed for the woods. Luckily, I have to drive only one mile from home to hunt.

When I arrived at my hunting location, I sprayed with scent killer, put on my armguard and gloves, and started toward my stand. I hadn't hunted from this particular stand for about two weeks, so I was a little excited, knowing the deer would not be expecting anyone to be there.

I moved through the woods slowly, trying to be extra quiet. I reached my stand, which is a ladder stand made of pipe with a wooden platform; a chain around the tree with a turnbuckle holds the stand tightly to the tree. I slowly started to climb the stand, but as I reached the last rung of the ladder the stand started to shake. Apparently, winds during the last two weeks had moved the tree, loosening the chain.

I lost my balance, but instead of falling backward and landing on my back, I ended up jumping off and landing on my feet. After I hit the ground, I rolled over and started to belt out a few cuss words. Then I looked down at my left leg, and saw that my left foot was sticking out at a severe angle. I knew right away that my ankle was broken.

The pain wasn't that bad, so I made up my mind to crawl the 150 yards back to my truck to get help. Luckily for me, the owner of the land had mowed down the brush and briers a few weeks earlier, so it was relatively easy to move through the forest.

When I reached the truck, it was really difficult to stand and get into the truck, but I knew I had to do it. Finally I was able to drive to the landowner's house. I blew the horn to summon help. The landowner's wife was home, and she took me to the hospital.

About five hours later, after surgery that included nine screws and a steel plate, I found out how bad it was. The doctor told me I would have to take about three months off work.

I want to use this story to tell all hunters to *check that stand* before climbing into it. Take a few minutes, look it over, grab and shake it and make sure it is tight to the tree. I sure wish I would have checked my stand before climbing into it, because that accident ended my deer hunting for the year. Next year, I am planning to hunt from the ground.

Remember this story the next time you are headed to your treestand. It happened to me … it could happen to you too!

Ray Redlin
Winama, IN

THE EXPERT'S NOTEBOOK

Dry Is Warm ... by Ron Spomer

Years of enduring and trying to avoid cold feet have taught me that dry equals warm. Once your insulating layer, whether socks or felt liner, gets wet, your feet get cold. The moisture constantly pulls heat from your tootsies. Ideally your feet should stay humid but your insulating layers dry.

Here are a few tactics to try:

1. Encase your feet in plastic. I started this with plastic bread bags years ago. Moist air trapped inside the bag signals your feet to reduce perspiration, having reached their humid comfort level. External socks stay dry to retain their insulating value. The only problem is that the plastic usually squeezes your toes uncomfortably once you pull your socks over it. Sharp toenails may tear the plastic as you walk. Applying talcum powder to your feet and to the bags before pulling on the bags and socks sometimes alleviates the first problem. Trimming toenails cures the latter. Still, this tactic is best reserved for stand hunting.

2. When walking, I've come to love Gore-Tex or Seal Skinz socks. They keep my feet dry and comfortable even in waders. Both pass moisture away from the foot, leaving dry sock material against it. Still, the passed moisture collects in the next insulating layer, reducing its thermal efficiency. Other options include polypropylene lined socks and similar hydrophobic sock materials combined with a breathable boot to force moisture out.

3. Another popular tactic is to apply antiperspirant liberally to the bottom of the foot, stopping or at least moderating sweat production. Another great idea is carrying spare socks and changing when your feet start to get cold. This, however, can be more than a slight hassle when snow is deep and the mercury is plunging. Still, it's usually worth the effort, and the dry insulation brings almost immediate relief.

RON SPOMER

Try these and other ideas you might come up with to keep your insulating layers dry. No one has invented the perfect "dry foot" for cold weather hunting yet, but there should be a combination of tactics that'll work for you.

Wind Judgment

To calculate the wind adjustment you'll need to make when taking a long-range shot, all you need is a little observation and some simple math.

Begin by observing the mirage coming off the earth. Note the angle of the mirage, then divide that number by four. Then calculate the distance to the target in yards and "move the decimal point" two digits to the left (so 300 yards becomes 3.00, or 3; 350 yards becomes 3.5 and so on). Multiply that number by the divided angle of mirage. Finally, divide that number by four. The result equals the number of "clicks" or half-minutes of angle that you need to adjust for windage. It's easier than it sounds, and really works.

Let's say the mirage is at a 45° angle. Divide 45 by four; the closest whole number is 11. Now let's say your target is 300 yards away. Multiply 11 by three (remember, move the decimal point in the yardage by two digits first), and you'll end up with 33. Now divide 33 by four, which is 8.25. Finally, round the number to the nearest whole number—eight. Adjust your aim by eight clicks.

This concept was the idea of Carlos Hathcock, a very successful military sharpshooter.

Greg Vretis
Jacksonville, FL

1 *Calculate the angle of the mirage at the target (45° in this case) and the distance to the target.*

2 *Divide the angle of mirage by 4; round to the nearest whole number.*

11.25 (round to 11)
4 ⟌ 45

3 *Move the decimal point in the distance reading by two digits.*

300 yds = 3.00

4 *Multiply the divided mirage number by the shortened distance figure.*

3.00 x 11 = 33

5 *Divide the resulting number by 4; this is the wind adjustment in "clicks."*

8.25 (round to 8)
4 ⟌ 33

Hunting with the Barometer

The son of a gunsmith, I grew up among hunters.

There were good ones and bad ones; the hard-luck hunters we all know, ones who occasionally got trophies, and hunters who produced consistently. Year after year I watched as those latter hunters harvested giant bucks and bull moose. At a young age, I learned which hunters to listen to, and which ones not to heed.

One tip that kept surfacing was about barometric pressure and its effect on game movement. All the productive hunters had different ways of watching the barometric pressure. Some had barometers in their homes; some said they knew when the pressure was falling because they would have pain in arthritic joints; some watched water levels rise and fall in their toilets; still others watched the smoke from their wood stoves emerge from the chimney and drop in a shroud around their cabins when pressure was falling.

Several years ago, I moved to a deer-rich area and began feeding the whitetails so I could watch them from my house. Deer began to arrive in droves. I was mildly disappointed, however, that most of the deer, especially the large bucks, were mostly nocturnal.

The normal routine was that minutes before dark, the deer started to show at my feeder, dusky unidentifiable shapes of all sizes. I have long known that whitetail deer are nocturnal and that increased human activity increases this trend, but there was still a mystery involved.

Occasionally, the deer would show several hours before nightfall. Why? A rapidly falling barometer? An impending snowstorm? *Yes!* Now that I had pieced the puzzle together, I began a log book and bought a barometer. The morning news would predict a snowstorm for the following day, and while the barometer fell steadily throughout the day, the deer, grouse, rabbits and even birds would feed early that day. At these times, I was treated to views of the biggest and best deer visiting my feeder in broad daylight.

I also noted that after a big snowfall, the game would hole up tight and there would be no tracks. Once the barometer rose, though, within 24 hours there would be tracks all over. But rest assured, they didn't show at my feeder during the day when the barometer was rising like this.

I am a hunting and fishing guide, and know that barometric pressure affects wildlife activity directly. Fish and game are triggered into heavy feeding patterns before storms, when the barometer is falling rapidly.

Once you start observing the barometer and game patterns, you will see proof over and over again that barometric pressure has a major impact on game movement.

Jim Mansell
Callander, ONT

SPECIAL
EXPERT ADVICE

quick tip

Water for Your Dog

When you are working with your gun dog in the field, natural sources of water may not be readily available. If you are training him in summer or hunting in early fall in hot, dry conditions, have a canteen or squirt bottle of water along. A folded aluminum sheet can be fashioned into a drinking bowl, or you can simply pull out your dog's lower lip and drip water from a canteen into his mouth.

Glenn Sapir
Shrub Oak, NY

quick tip

Give Yourself the Advantage

When backpack hunting, I make sure to set up my camp on the downwind side and at least a half-mile away from the pocket I think holds the game I'm hunting. This keeps the animals from inadvertently seeing, hearing or smelling me or my camp, and also allows me to move into position before first light in the morning, without them ever knowing I'm around.

When that sun does come up, make sure you set up so that the sun will be at your back or quartering off your rear shoulder when you're glassing. This eliminates glare on your optic lenses, making it easier for you to see. It also forces the game to look right into the sun, making it almost impossible for them to see you.

Bob Robb
Valdez, AK

Respect All Animals

While hunting for mule deer in Spanish Fork Canyon, Utah (our favorite spot), my son Eric and I were both noticing lots of fresh sign from our quarry. We were still-hunting, and hoping to bag a nice buck. Even though we were quite a ways apart, we both noticed that the deer sign ended abruptly. Puzzled, we arrived at our meeting spot and decided to head straight up the north ridge of the mountain we had been hunting to learn more about it.

The terrain was steep, rocky and brushy. As we were nearing the summit plateau I bent down to go under a tree branch … and saw a big, fresh cougar track staring back at me. Ahead of me was a small cave in the rocks, where this print and others like it were directed. Eric was just behind me and whispered, "Dad, we're on a cougar track!"

We agreed to back out of the immediate area quietly and quickly. Lower down the mountain we talked about it, and agreed that we didn't want to create a situation that might cause us to shoot an animal unnecessarily or, maybe, in the steep, close quarters of the cat's domain, get injured ourselves. We have a responsibility as woodsmen and hunters to all of nature.

Layne T. Oliver
West Valley, UT

THE EXPERT'S NOTEBOOK

Carry Two Cameras ...
by Jim Shockey

On that once-in-a-lifetime hunt, carry two cameras. Why would you save for years, plan for months and travel for days, yet risk having your camera (the thing that will preserve your memories of the adventure) break down? Buy a second camera. Better yet, buy one with a different power lens and make sure you use it as much as you use your regular camera. Without doubt, you'll get some great pictures with each camera. That's the bonus. If one camera breaks down, you'll still have a slide show for your buddies!

Three Useful Knots Every Hunter Should Know

Here are a few easy-to-learn knots that can come in very handy when you're hunting.

The first is called the Waggoner's Hitch (also called Trucker's Hitch or Power Cinch). Use this to lift a log off the trail, to tie gear on a car rack, or anywhere you need a powerful, tight, pulley-like system. The rope going off the top of the illustration is already tied off to something secure, like a tree. Make the fixed loop as shown, wrap the free end around the object to be lifted or secured, then run it through the loop; pull to lift the object (or tighten). If you're using this knot to tie something down, finish off the free end with a secure knot.

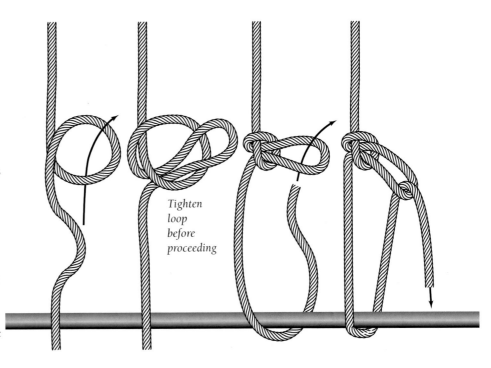

Tighten loop before proceeding

At left is the Transom Knot. Use this to lash two poles or sticks together (for example, when building a quick, temporary structure). This also works well to quickly secure canoe paddles or oars to the car's luggage rack. This knot is a bit hard to untie, but you can get it loose with patience. Many people take the easy way out and simply cut across the center of the knot at an angle; this frees both ends.

At right is the Highwayman's Hitch (also called the Draw Hitch). Use this quick-release hitch to temporarily tie your dog or horse to a tree or post, or any place you need a temporary fastening. Tension on the tied end will not cause the knot to loosen, but a pull on the tag end frees the knot instantly.

Teresa Marrone
Minneapolis, MN

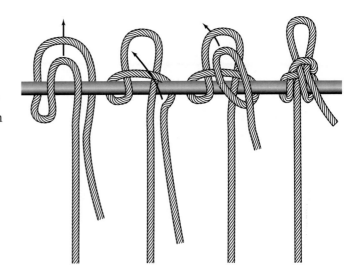

The Expert's Notebook

Keep a Hunting Record
... by Glenn Sapir

Having a record of every hunt you make can provide a variety of dividends. Not only will it make great reading and help you relive wonderful memories, but it can provide excellent reference material that will help you match up likely locations, times for action and strategies with your current situation.

Try to stay on top of the record keeping while the hunt is fresh in your mind. Create and copy a standard form and store each form in a three-ring binder. Your form might include the following headings: Date; base camp; location hunted; type of terrain; companions; weather; hunting tools used; time hunt began; time hunt ended; shots taken (number, time, distance); misses; hits; game harvested (species, number, gender, physical statistics—weight, antler/horn specs, etc.); other wildlife seen (species, number, time, what it was they were doing); companions' experiences; and other noteworthy aspects of the hunt.

GLENN SAPIR

We've all seen the photos of hunters proudly displaying a buck with blazing green eyes from the use of flash. To eliminate this "green eye" syndrome, visit a taxidermist and buy a pair of taxidermy deer eyes. These half-moon glass eyes can be easily slipped over the real eyes and mimic the look of a live deer's eyes without the green reflection. I've used the same eyes for mule deer, whitetail deer, pronghorn and even elk.

Mark Kayser
Pierre, SD

Don't Leave the Camera Behind

There's a small item that every hunter should have in his or her pack but often doesn't: a camera. There is no better picture of a successful hunt than one taken right where it took place. A picture of an animal lying in the front yard or in the bed of a pickup truck doesn't have the same impact as one of a buck with the autumn woods as a backdrop or of a big gobbler on your favorite ridge on a bright spring morning.

Since many hunters hunt by themselves, they make the excuse that no one was there to take their picture. They're missing out on what might be their one chance to get the photo of a lifetime. Many small, moderately-priced cameras have timers on them and work well for self-portraits.

I use an Advantix camera. It can be set up in a variety of positions using either a small tripod or various woodland features including stumps, fenceposts, blowdowns or small ridges.

I am far from being a professional photographer, but you would be amazed at some of the photos I've taken while hunting by myself. Trust me, your own hunting photos will take on a whole new meaning if you do this too.

Another tip is to position your animal where it shows up best. Typically this will be out of the shadows and facing into the sun. This is especially true when photographing wild turkeys. The blue and red head, bronze feathers and barred wings make a great photo. If you happen to get your bird coming off the roost, it's well worth it to wait until the sun comes up enough to show off the bird's colors.

Savor your moment in the woods when you have the chance, and put a little extra effort into preserving your memories. Don't make the mistake of taking your time for granted (and we are all guilty of this from time to time).

We owe it to ourselves and our children to get them interested in hunting and the outdoors; what better way than through your own photos and stories?

So the next time you're thinking of buying more hunting gear because it's a new kind of camo or something that your buddy has, put it back on the shelf and spend the money on a quality camera. The results will last a lifetime.

Mike Winka
Flora, IL

quick tip

Don't Lose Your Gear

Attach a 6- to 8-inch length of bright-colored surveyor's tape to your camera, binoculars, game saw and hunting knife. This will reduce the chances of losing them when you are outdoors.

Charles Horejsi
Missoula, MT

A Handful of Fire-Starting Tips

Here's a homemade fire starter that is easy to make, and really works great. In a clean, empty coffee can, melt a pound of paraffin wax. Using a needle nose pliers, carefully slip in a whole roll of toilet paper. Use the pliers to turn and roll the paper in the wax until the paper is completely saturated and the wax has been absorbed. Remove the roll with the pliers, but be careful because the roll is very hot! Let the roll cool and harden, then cut it into lengthwise wedges. These wedges can then be cut into thinner slices; a piece the size of a nickel is all you need to get that early morning campfire going! They can be carried in your pocket for an emergency fire, and start easily even when wet.

Once I'm in camp, I also make a number of fuzz sticks. This old-timer's trick works as well today as when your grandfather was in knickers. Use your knife to peel shavings on all four corners of a stick of kindling, leaving the shavings still attached to the stick. You can make a number of these any time you're sitting around the fire, so they're ready when you need them.

To build a fire, I lay the fire starter down first, and top it with two or three fuzz sticks. Then I add kindling and the larger wood. I lay my fires before my afternoon hunt, so when I return after dark, wet and cold, all I need do is touch a match to the fire starter. Before I turn in for the evening, I get everything ready for the morning, so I can quickly assemble and light the fire in the morning.

Norm Schertenleib
Choteau, MT

FROM THE EXPERT'S NOTEBOOK

Don't Forget These in Your Daypack ... by Tom Carpenter

Like many big game hunters, I take a daypack or fanny pack along on every outing, whether I'm hunting whitetails a hill or two behind the barns, stalking antelope on the prairie or climbing at timberline for mulies.

Everyone has their list of what they're willing to carry along, but here's something from my list that you might not otherwise think of: an extra pair of socks. They weigh hardly anything, so are not a burden to add to the pack.

At midday, with your feet all tired and sweaty, a fresh pair of socks can be a real pick-me-up and energizer for the rest of the day. And of course, if your feet get wet for any reason, they will more than welcome a pair of clean, dry socks. Take care of tired, sweaty, damp or downright wet feet. Fresh socks make it easy; you'll feel better and hunt harder.

Here's another tip that may save you some headaches in the woods. If your flashlight batteries have ever died when you're a mile and a half back in a swamp looking for your Opening Day deer stand, you know how frustrating it is to fumble around and replace them in the dark. Your batteries are dead and it's pitch black, so you have no light to work by! (Guess who this has happened to.) The biggest problem is figuring out the orientation of the positive and negative ends of the batteries, and how they should go together in the flashlight.

Here's the solution I use now. Take your extra batteries out of the packaging and use electrician's tape or duct tape to secure them together in the orientation needed for the flashlight. Then store them in an accessible spot in your daypack, fanny pack or pocket. They'll slide in quickly and easily, and you'll be back on the trail quickly.

Protect Your Hearing

After a lifetime of being exposed to gunfire, my hearing is just not as good as it used to be. To protect the hearing I have left, I now wear earplugs, especially when I have time to set up a shot. I use the disposable foam earplugs, but I've found that the paper envelopes they are packaged in don't last but a minute or two in my pocket while hunting. I came up with an easy solution. I poked a hole in the lid and bottom of an empty 35mm film canister, then ran a short length of parachute cord through each hole and tied it off with knots. Now I have a cheap case that lasts and keeps my earplugs clean.

Michael C. Thompson
Border, AK

THE EXPERT'S NOTEBOOK

HELP: Life-Saving Advice ... by Glenn Sapir

If you are waterfowling and your boat capsizes, hypothermia — the life-threatening lowering of your body core temperature — becomes an immediate threat. Assuming you are wearing a personal flotation device, but you can't get back into the boat or reach shore, you can delay the onset of hypothermia by assuming the Heat Escape Lessening Position (HELP).

Cross your ankles, place your arms across your chest, draw your knees into your abdomen and lean back. This can halve body heat loss in cold water. Two or more persons should assume the huddle position by placing their arms around each other and maintaining chest-to-chest contact.

FROM THE EXPERT'S NOTEBOOK

Wilderness Tips ... by Jim Shockey

Safety—Sadly, I cannot count on two hands the number of my peers who've died as a result of "get-home-itis." In our modern world, we live by schedules and important dates. Our whole day is divided into lunch breaks, dinner breaks, coffee breaks and days off, and quite frankly, it works ... or rather, it works in the civilized lands. Out in the wild lands, living by schedules is a killer. Nature decides when and if you can travel to make an appointment. Nature decides if you're going to get out of the mountains to be at your son's or daughter's graduation. Remember that when you're stuck in camp after your hunt and can't fly out because of inclement weather. The weather will change; don't push your outfitter to fly you out before it does. Sit tight like the Inuit of the Arctic; home is exactly where you are when bad weather strikes.

Attitude—Preconceived ideas are best left at home when you go on a wilderness hunt; especially preconceived ideas about food. On a wilderness hunt, food is anything that will keep you alive and functioning, period. On one hunt, we horsebacked for two days into a camp only to discover that all the meat left there (hanging in the trees) had been compromised by flies. No big deal; we simply cut the egg- and maggot-covered parts off and dined away! The same goes for what constitutes food. Here at home, I'd gag before I'd eat a dirty little gopher, but up on the mountain? Some of the finest meals I've had have included dirty little gopher bits in what would otherwise have been

WILD BLUEBERRIES

quick tip

Be Ready for Wild Blueberries

I carry a couple of zip-top bags in my pack so if I find a good patch of wild berries while hunting, I can pick some and bring them home. It's quite a treat to have a wild berry pie after your game dinner. Just be sure you know what you are picking so you don't poison yourself!

Michael C. Thompson Border, AK

Cold-Weather Gun Tip

If you're out hunting in extremely cold conditions, remove all the oil from your gun and replace it with graphite. This will keep moving parts from freezing.

Jeremy Evers, Burns, OR

quick tip

No-Fail Fire Starter

Interested in a reliable and highly effective emergency fire starter? Purchase a cassette torch. They are built around a disposable lighter and generate a flame temperature of about 2,350°F. They have enough firepower to set even damp wood afire. They sell for about $12 in most hardware stores.

Charles Horejsi
Missoula, MT

Some Handy Signals for Hunters

Over the years, my husband and I have spent a lot of time spot-and-stalk hunting for antelope in Wyoming. It can take quite a while to walk to the area where we've spotted a group of animals, and by the time we're approaching their presumed location we don't know how close they are, or where the bucks are within the group. Sometimes, one person may creep up a hill while the other remains below, waiting for information. Also, it often happens that one person can see something the other can't, due to topography, cover or our individual positions.

Rather than creep back down the hill or to an area where we can discuss the situation, we've developed a set of simple hand signals that help us communicate silently with each other. If we're any distance apart, we watch each other's hand signals through our binoculars.

First, we indicate how many animals are out there (or how many we are concerned with, anyway). This one's easy: hold up one finger for one, two fingers for two and so on. To describe a herd, open and close the hand several times rapidly, going from a fist to a full "five open fingers" position.

One of the most important things we want to identify is the locations of bucks versus does, and in particular, big bucks. For a buck, we raise one hand with two fingers in a "V" (like the old "victory sign" or the "peace sign" of the '60s); the two fingers are curved slightly to resemble horns. To identify a doe, we hold out

three fingers but point them down (think "cow's udder" ... okay, I know, antelope and deer don't look like that, but trust me, this works well!). If the buck is small-ish, hold the hand out flat, palm down and fingers spread, and rock it back and forth to convey "so-so"; for a big buck, a pumping fist gets the message across.

If the herd or animal is close, we then hold our thumb and fingers together fairly close, as though indicating "just a little bit." The farther the animals are, the wider we spread our thumb and fingers.

It's easy to see how this sort of communication can be expanded. You can describe contour such as hills, valleys, creekbeds, and so on, with simple hand motions. You can also give your partner a quick indication of your plans; for example, you can tell your partner that you're going to go around a knoll to the right while s/he should follow a creekbed to the left. All of this communication is completely silent, so the animals never know you're just on the other side of the hill. It's a great tactic to use when you want to keep the edge of surprise on your side.

Teresa Marrone
Minneapolis, MN

Making Life Better at Camp

Here are two tips to help make your time at camp or the cabin more enjoyable.

- If you are using a generator, dig a pit several feet deep to put it in. This really cuts down on the noise made by the generator.

- Bring a bag of lye to camp for the outhouse. If sprinkled into the pit daily, it really cuts down on flies and odor.

Jeremy Evers
Burns, OR

THE EXPERT'S NOTEBOOK

Camera Wrap for Binoculars ...
by Mark Kayser

Having binoculars bouncing and pounding on my chest while hunting irritates me, especially when I'm moving quickly on game. So far, I haven't been satisfied with any of the elastic-style devices that are sold to alleviate this problem.

Instead, I discovered that several camera companies make a large neoprene wrap that firmly wraps around your body to hold a camera snugly against your chest. It works great for binoculars too. The neoprene is wide enough to cover the eyepieces and protect the entire binoculars from scratches, dust and moisture. Not only does it keep the binoculars tucked against my chest when I'm moving, but it keeps them out of the way when I'm drawing an arrow or shooting my rifle.

quick tip

Something's Afoot in the Wind

In the damp coastal climate that I have to guide in, I've found the very best wind indicator to be "foot powder" of whatever brand. Because of the chemical makeup of this powder, in wet weather, it doesn't lump up inside the container or clog up the openings of the container. Also, the plastic container it comes in has a couple dozen holes in the top, not a single hole like some wind indicator bottles. This also prevents clogging. More importantly, when my eyes are focused on the bear I'm stalking, I can give the container a shake and a large volume of powder comes out—enough so I can see which way it is floating without taking my eyes off the bear.

Jim Shockey
Duncan, BC

quartering • field care • cooking tips • mounting

FINAL FLOURISHES

The hunt's work doesn't end when you make a successful shot. The responsible hunter ensures that trophies and meat are properly cared for, to make maximum use of the resource and to extend the life of the hunt.

In this final chapter, you'll learn special finishing techniques, including how to mount a turkey cape, how to bone your own deer and how to make a European-style skull mount. And there are lots of other tips that will help you make the most of your hard-won game.

Don't Wait—Get to the Taxidermist

In the past three or four years, our hunting time in the northeast has brought us some pretty warm weather, which can create some problems for hunters who want to have their deer head mounted.

The typical scenario is that a hunter has shot a trophy buck, and is very proud of it. He wants to show it off to his hunting buddies, so he drives around here and there, visiting friends. Two or three days later, he brings the trophy to the taxidermist in a plastic bag, who examines the trophy and explains that the cape is no longer in a condition to be mounted. There are several things you can do to prevent this tragedy from happening to you.

First, on the same day you harvest your trophy, get the deer checked in and then head straight to the taxidermist to have it caped. The longer the hide stays on, the lesser your chances of ending up with a useable cape.

Second, if you cape the deer yourself, never put the cape in a plastic bag. Plastic is the taxidermist's worst enemy, because it holds heat in. Instead, put the cape in burlap or a feed sack. The only time a plastic bag is acceptable is when the cape is going directly from the deer into the freezer.

The moral is, if you want to show off your buck to your friends and neighbors, either take a picture or wait until the taxidermist has mounted it. This is especially important if the weather is warm. Don't let your trophy get ruined; get it to the taxidermist!

Mike Moriarty
Bloomington, IN

Handy Field-Dressing Kit

I live in southern Arizona and do most of my hunting here. I don't need to tell you how important water is to a hunter in our desert. I put together an inexpensive field-dressing packet which not only conserves water, but also helps keep our hands clean.

In a zip-top sandwich bag, I enclose a pair of latex gloves and a packet or two of moist towelettes. When field dressing the game, the gloves keep our hands clean, and instead of wasting drinking water to clean hands, we use the towelettes. When done, we just place the used gloves and towelettes in the sandwich bag and carry it back to camp for proper disposal.

Joe M. Chavez
Douglas, AZ

Quartering Elk in the Field

If you've ever taken an elk in the back-country, you know you'll have to quarter it to pack it out. But many hunters have never dealt with an animal this size before and don't know where to start. A friend showed me this easy method:

Norm Schertenleib
Choteau, MT

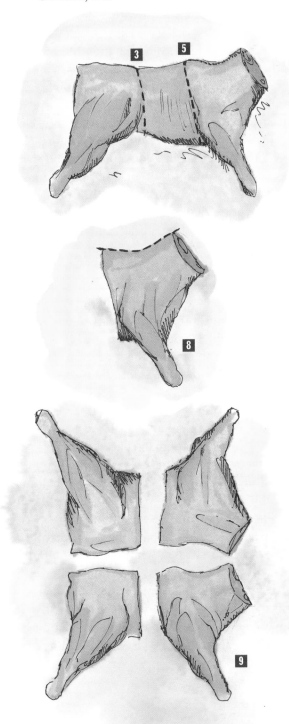

1 When gutting the elk, cut open the chest cavity all the way to the neck. This way, the windpipe and guts can be pulled out in one motion.

2 After gutting and skinning the elk, cut down the flanks to the ball joint, where the rear legs join the backbone.

3 Saw through the ball joint, separating the hindquarters from the carcass.

4 Now cut through the spine to the tail, dividing the two hindquarters.

5 For the middle, locate the rib that's right behind the elbow. Cut along this rib, detaching the ribcage from the front quarters.

6 Bone out the loin, tenderloin and rib meat, then discard the ribcage.

7 Since the breastbone has been split, it's easy to finish up the front quarters. Cut off the head.

8 Position the front quarters with the spine facing up and the legs out to the sides; cut through the spine, separating the front quarters.

9 All four quarters are ready to pack out, and no meat has been wasted.

Taking Care of Your Big Game ... After the Shot

PHASE I: INITIAL EFFORTS AFTER THE SHOT

You've taken your best shot, and are sure you connected. Now what do you do? First stop and think as objectively as you can. Flag the exact spot you are standing before you move an inch! Now determine exactly where the animal was standing when you took the shot, and pick a landmark (tree, bush, rock, trail turn) to mark the spot before you move.

Now you have to decide on a controversial point: pursue the animal and flag the landmark, or wait for a period of time to allow the animal to expire prior to pursuit. This point depends on many things, including the type of weapon and the caliber of ammunition you are using, the position and body language of the animal, the reactions to the shot(s), terrain, etc. This is the point when every hunter must rely on his or her skill, knowledge and hunting partners. The best piece of advice I can offer is to seriously and objectively look at the actions and reactions that have occurred and make a good decision based on the best information available.

Once you've flagged the two reference points (after the waiting period), it is time to track the animal, hopefully not too far. Assume nothing! Assume you are tracking a live, non-wounded animal. Do not relax and run in without caution, expecting to find an animal laying there stone dead. This is the mistake of both the novice and expert hunter. You need as much skill after the shot as you did in order to make the shot. Follow the blood trail or tracks and flag each directional turn of the animal. On the final approach to a downed animal you've sighted, look it over carefully. Use your binoculars or scope to ensure that another shot is not needed. Approach the animal assuming that you will need to make another shot. Have your weapon at the ready until you can touch the animal on the eyeball with it from the side opposite the legs.

Now that your animal is down, you need to tag it and recall or review all regulations prior to field dressing. Are you required to leave trace of sex ID attached to the animal? Where is the tag required to be placed? Some states require the tag to be directly attached to the largest portion of the carcass that will be transported.

PHASE II: REMOVING THE INTERNAL ORGANS

The first step in beginning the process is to consider how your animal is positioned. I have found that placing the hind end of the animal downhill is the easiest position to work with. It may be necessary to tie the front end or head of the animal to a tree in order to keep it on the slope in steep country. Before gutting the animal, cut out around the rectum until you can tie the end of it off with a shoestring or other suitable material. This simple step will reduce the possibility of fecal contamination of the meat.

To remove the internal organs, start at the point where the belly comes back into the groin area. Carefully part the belly hair and make a few gentle knife strokes to cut through the external muscles until the white connective tissue of the stomach can be seen through the cut. Now put one hand inside the carcass and push the stomach back into the body cavity to guide your knife with. Cutting from the inside of the body cavity will help keep your knife sharp for the chore ahead, and also prevents the stomach contents from getting on your carcass. Work up the body cavity until you reach the sternum. At this point, the stomach and internal organs should be partially out of the body cavity. Split the sternum by cutting through the cartilage in the center, using either your knife or a saw.

Your goal is to remove the internal organs as "one piece" without cutting into the stomach, bile duct or bladder. Reach into the carcass and cut away the windpipe, lungs and heart. Work your way down to the diaphragm and cut it loose as well. Now pull the internal organs out of the carcass toward the rear end until you reach the rectum area. You will need to carefully cut around the rectum internally until the entire tract is free. Inspect the following during field dressing of the carcass: liver, lungs, heart and lymph nodes. Look for discoloration, spots or swollen lymph nodes. Carefully inspect all injuries for gross infection and off-odors. If you have any doubts about the animal, contact the local game and fish department for an advisory of any potentially dangerous situations that may be affecting the area. They can advise you if the meat is safe to eat.

PHASE III: SKINNING AND QUARTERING

With the animal properly field-dressed, it's time to slow down and care for the meat. Remove the hide from the carcass to allow for faster cooling. Removing the hide can drop the temperature of the carcass significantly. It may not always be practical to remove the hide from the carcass in the field, but it should be removed as soon as possible. Begin skinning at the rear end of the animal by cutting from the inside of the hide to the outside and splitting open the hide on the hind leg. Carefully skin the hindquarter until it is exposed entirely. Continue from the loin and rib area, pulling the hide across the carcass towards the back. Split the hide (again from the inside out) and expose the front quarter.

Cut the tendons across the break joints and snap off or saw through the legs, leaving the major tendons intact to hang the quarters from. Tie on the rope to hang up the quarters with before detaching the quarters. Hang the quarters and cover them in good quality game bags. Remove the meat from the rib and neck areas and put it in a game bag. Cut out and discard all badly bruised and bloodshot areas from the carcass; this meat is not edible and should not be processed with the rest of the carcass.

If you are able to leave the loin and back areas intact to hang them, proceed at this point to the other two quarters, working until the loin and back area can be lifted and tied up with the quarters. Be sure to remove the tenderloins from the inside of the carcass in the loin area, taking care to not damage the high quality meat.

PHASE IV: TAKING CARE OF THE HARD-EARNED MEAT

After your meat is covered and hung to cool, you need to watch the thermometer. The ideal temperature to keep your meat is lower than 40°F (5°C). This temperature inhibits the growth of most spoilage bacteria and molds and will give you the highest quality meat. Have the meat processed as soon as possible after the harvest. Most waste occurs due to neglecting the post-harvest carcass.

If your elk is to be processed by a meat cutter, ask/answer the following: Will my meat be processed in a batch with other carcasses? What is the carcass weight? Do you want bone in or out of the steaks and roasts? If having cooked or processed products (jerky, pepperoni, summer sausage, salami, German sausage, Polish sausage, etc.) made from your meat, what is the expected percentage return after processing, how is it to be packaged, in what sizes, and what percentage of tallow is added to the ground meat? It is a good idea to contact the local game processors before you go into the field, to find out what services and facilities are available to you before you hunt. This will prevent you from wasting any of the hard-earned meat.

Craig H. Doan
Weiser, ID

ABOVE: Dave Brown (left) and Craig Doan (right) with 6×6 bull elk taken in North Idaho's panhandle.

FROM THE EXPERT'S NOTEBOOK

After the Shot: Caring for Birds ... by Chris Winchester

Here are some tips for field dressing waterfowl and upland game birds, in the field and at home.

FIELD DRESSING: Equipment: Small knife, paper towels

1. Cut the skin below the breast bone to expose the entrails.

2. Make a short slit above the breast toward the chin. Pull out the windpipe. Remove the crop and any undigested food it contains.

3. Remove the entrails, including lungs, heart, gizzard, etc. Wipe cavity with paper towels.

AT-HOME DRESSING: When you get home, there are many ways to clean birds.

Wet Plucking:

The easiest way is to hold the bird under a running faucet, then dip the bird several times in simmering (160°-180°F) water. Rub the feathers with your thumb and they should strip off easily, especially if you are wet-plucking upland birds. Waterfowl is a bit more difficult to wet-pluck; add a little dish soap to the water to help saturate feathers, and be sure to rinse well afterwards. With upland birds or waterfowl, after the feathers have been stripped away, cut off the head, tail and feet, and pat the bird dry.

Dry Plucking:

Grasp a few feathers at a time and pull. Use pliers to pull wing and tail feathers. Then use a burner or torch to singe off any downy feathers or hair. Afterward, remove head, legs, etc.

Waxing Waterfowl:

Heat a large pot of water to boiling. Melt several cakes of paraffin in the water; you should have a layer of wax that is 3/8-inch thick.

1. Rough-pluck large feathers from the body.

2. Dip the bird in the melted wax and water, then slowly remove the bird. Hold the bird in the air until the wax dries.

3. Peel the hardened wax from the bird. The feathers will be stripped away with the wax. You can re-use the wax by re-melting and straining it.

FREEZING

I prefer to freeze my birds in water. I normally place the cleaned birds in a zip-top bag, then fill it with water until the birds are covered. Then, I just seal and freeze.

Fine Dining: Grouse at Camp

I hunt from a camp and usually spend a week above 3,000 feet in a tent in New York's Catskill Mountains. Ruffed grouse is *the* premier wild game meat when it's not deer or turkey season.

I think I can taste the difference between apple-fed and pine-fed grouse, and I try to enhance the apple flavor when I can. The first step to premier taste is to hang the bird. The French are known for hanging game birds until the meat would be considered spoiled by most Americans, and I don't go for that amount of hanging either. But an overnight hang, if the temperature permits, adds a good flavor to the meat. If the meat would freeze overnight (or spoil for that matter), then you can't hang it.

A friend of mine who's a French chef taught me to pluck the bird without peeling the skin off. Grouse, like most game birds, don't have much (if any) fat, and the skin will help keep the meat moist. I also like to stuff my spices under the skin.

The spices I use to cook the grouse are easily available in my hunting area. I use a combination of wild thyme, thorn apples and wild leeks. In addition to the "wild" herbs, I use salt, pepper and bacon.

I don't crush the wild thyme, because I like the way it looks whole. I stuff the cavity with wild leeks (or onions if I can't find leeks), wild thyme, thorn berries, salt and pepper. Then I wrap the bird in thyme and bacon. If red peppers are in season, I add some of those to the stuffing.

In camp, for dinner, I grill the whole birds as described, cooking them slowly over a warming fire. It takes 30 to 60 minutes to cook the birds over this low fire, but they stay juicy because the fire doesn't dry them out.

If I plan to take the birds home, I bone the meat. Then I use the same seasonings, adding them to a sweet white wine; I marinate the boneless breasts and the drumsticks in this mixture.

I don't use measurements, and I recommend that you cook to your individual tastes as well. For example, I like garlic sometimes with the grouse, but it isn't to everyone's taste. There are plenty of spice blends that can enhance the meal, so experiment to find the flavors you prefer. One last word about cooking in camp: If you use spring water for cooking, always boil for 10 to 20 minutes first to avoid "beaver fever."

Terry M. Staub
Treadwell, NY

Versatile Gloves for Field Dressing

When field dressing any large animal, from antelope to moose, wear long over-the-elbow disposable gloves (available from your vet or farm supply store). Take out the tenderloins, and even the back-strap if you have to; then, while still holding onto the meat, turn the gloves inside out so the meat is inside the gloves. This keeps the meat clean until you get home. Also, always carry gallon-sized zip-top freezer bags in your backpack for the heart and liver.

Kate Hoppe
Powell, WY

Limited-Space Turkey Mount

If you've bagged a nice turkey but have limited space, or you simply don't wish to pay the mounting charges (which can be $350 or more), here's how to make a wall mount at home.

You'll need the following:
- Sharp knife
- Large piece of cardboard
- Borax (look in the laundry aisle at the supermarket for this)
- Glue
- Decorative nails
- Panel (optional but highly recommended)
- Balmex, if you wish to use the wings (see below)
- Tanning oil or neat's-foot oil

I prefer a panel for turkey mounts. The panel makes it easy to move the mount from one location to another without damaging the skin. Check with a taxidermy supply house for panels; you can also have a local cabinet maker custom-make a panel for you, or make your own if you're handy with wood.

As to the Balmex: this non-poisonous embalming fluid can be injected into the fleshy areas that are hard to skin. It's ideal for wings, tail and feet. Like the panel, Balmex can be ordered from a taxidermy supply company. (I can recommend Van Dyke's, P.O. Box 278, Woonsocket, SD 57388; 605-796-4425.)

After the kill, keep the feathers as free from blood and dirt as possible. Hang the gobbler by the head. Remove the wings, beard and feet. Start skinning where the feathers begin at the neck. Skin down the back and both sides; you can pull down with light pressure as you skin, but don't pull too hard or you may tear the cape.

Skin the cape to the base of the tail, then remove the tail from the body, keeping the tail attached to the cape. Working from the

underside, slit the skin and remove all the meat from the tail, then rub borax into the skin, or inject Balmex into the tail.

Place the cape and tail on the cardboard, skin-side up. Remove all bits of meat from the cape. Secure the cape and tail to the cardboard with decorative nails, stretching the skin tightly as you go. Rub a generous amount of borax into the skin. Put the cut end of the beard into a container of borax also, or inject the meat at the base of the beard with Balmex. If you wish to use the wings, inject them with Balmex and spread them on another piece of cardboard, arranging them in the position you wish to display them.

Let the mount dry for three or four weeks. Dump the excess borax from the mount; you can use a hair dryer set on low heat to blow away remaining borax. Now rub the skin side with tanning oil or neats-foot oil, and the cape is ready to attach to the panel.

A dab of glue will hold the beard in place—a hot-glue gun works great if you have one, but all-purpose glue works also. I have also used a brass casing from a shotgun shell to mount the beard; I filled the casing with caulking, put the beard in and let it dry, then attached it to the panel with an

eye-screw. If I'm displaying the feet, I use eye-screws to attach them to the panel.

For the final touch, have a small brass plaque made with your name, date and other information; you can go to a jewelry store or trophy shop to get a plaque like this. You may also wish to attach a photo from the hunt. This type of mount not only saves space, it is beautiful no matter how you do it.

Kenneth W. Crummett
Sugar Grove, WV

ILLUSTRATION ON OPPOSITE PAGE: *Slit the skin over the underside of the tail and scrape away all meat; or, inject the tail with Balmex.*
ILLUSTRATION AT LEFT: *If mounting wings, spread them on the drying board as you want them, then secure with tacks. Inject Balmex into meaty areas (shown in pink).*

For the Best Eating—Bone Your Deer at Home

Over many years of working with venison and other wild game, I've developed one hard-and-fast rule: I always bone big game rather than using traditional bone-in butchering methods. There are a number of benefits to this practice, starting with what's perhaps the most important: better-tasting meat.

In traditional butchery, the skinned carcass is cut up with a meat saw. As the saw cuts through muscle and bone, several things happen that adversely affect the flavor of the meat. First, strong-tasting fat or glands within the meat become part of the final cut. Second, as the saw cuts through bone, it smears bone marrow over the meat. This fatty substance carries a strong flavor in game animals and most hunters find it objectionable. Even when frozen, fat and marrow become rancid fairly quickly (fat doesn't freeze well, which is why you can't store sausages, oily fish or fatty meats as long as lean cuts), so meat that has fat will pick up an off-flavor more quickly than will boneless, trimmed meat.

Boned meat is easier to wrap for the freezer. You don't have to worry about jagged bone poking a hole in the wrap, exposing the meat to freezer burn. Plus, boneless meat takes up less freezer space than bone-in meat does, simply because the bulky bones have been removed.

Many butchers offer boning as an option when processing deer. However, I prefer to do it myself. I've watched butchers bone deer, and they can't afford to spend as much time fussing over it as I do. As an example, when boning the hind leg, many butchers simply make one long cut to remove the bone, then cut across the various muscle groups to make roasts. I don't think this cooks as nicely as a whole-muscle roast; plus, glands and fat remain in the roast unless

you break the muscle groups apart to remove them. I prefer to separate the hind leg into individual muscles; each becomes a boneless roast.

It's easiest to work as a team when boning a deer. One person handles the carcass breakdown, while the other bones the individual portions as they come off. Keep the meat cold at all times; if you can't bone a portion right away, wrap it in plastic wrap and refrigerate until you're ready.

Cutting up the Carcass

We hang our deer by the hindquarters, so the front legs are the first to come off. They are easy to remove, since there's no ball joint at the shoulder. Stand facing the chest cavity, and push one front leg

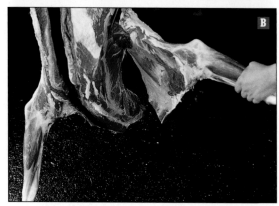

away from the animal's body. Cut between the leg and the ribcage (photo A), working your way toward the backbone until you can cut the shoulder away completely (photo B).

While one person bones out the front legs, the other can remove the loins and trim the ribs. The loin—also called the backstrap—is a long strip of meat that runs along the backbone on the outside of the deer; there's one on each side of the backbone. This is some of the best meat on the deer, so it pays to trim as close to the bone as possible.

Begin removing one loin by starting near the rump (if you have hung the deer by the head, start near the neck). Slide the tip of the knife between the loin and the ridge in the center of the backbone (this ridge is called the *chine*). Work the knife along the chine, scraping and cutting the meat away from the bone; the tip of the knife will stop where it hits the tops of the rib bones. Cut along the chine between the rump and the neck. To finish removing the loin,

You're now left with two rear legs connected at the spine, a cleaned-off backbone, and a neck. Cut off the neck, which can be boned, roasted whole or used for stock; cut the backbone into chunks for the stockpot.

Separating the rear legs is a bit tricky because they are connected to the pelvic bone with a ball joint. Cut close to the pelvic bone until you can see the round white ball at the end of the leg bone (photo F); you'll also see a cup in the pelvic bone where this ball rotates. Work your knife tip into this cup and separate the ball joint (photo G).

make a second cut, at a right angle to the first, along the rib tops toward the chine (photo C). Repeat with the loin on the other side (photo D).

The tenderloins are two smaller muscles you'll find on the inside of the body cavity, along the backbone near the rump. Many hunters remove the tenderloins at deer camp; they're best when eaten fresh. But if you didn't do this, remove them now before proceeding. Slip your knife underneath each tenderloin and scrape/cut it away from the backbone.

The ribs are next. Many hunters simply bone out the meat between the ribs to grind for burger, but savvy game cooks know that venison ribs are excellent eating. Most butchers don't offer to save the ribs when they process deer (I even had one try to argue with me when I asked him to do it); so this

is a real advantage in doing it yourself.

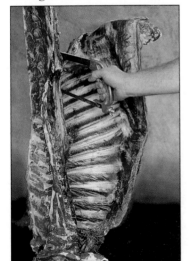

A small hunter's meat saw works best for this, although you can use a clean hacksaw. Cut the flank meat between the hind leg and the bottom of the ribcage; then, insert your saw and cut the ribs off next to the backbone (photo E shows the second side of ribs being removed).

You're almost done! Now just continue to cut the leg from the pelvic bone until it is free. A note of caution: the hind legs are heavy, and they will swing apart wildly when you free the leg from the pelvic bone. Enlist the help of someone to steady the legs as you cut. It's easiest to remove the pelvic bone

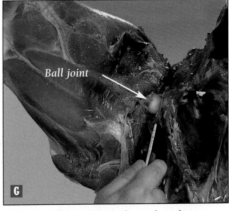

Ball joint

from the second leg on the cutting board rather than while the leg is still hanging.

On the following pages, you'll learn how to bone the various portions. Be sure to keep the portions cold until you complete boning.

Continued …

Boning the Front Quarters

The front leg is the first piece to come off the carcass (if you hang the deer from the hindquarters as I do), so we'll start there. A stiff-backed boning knife, with a fairly narrow tip, works best for most boning.

When you become your own butcher, you also need to learn about the characteristics of meat from various parts of the animal. Venison cuts are similar to beef cuts as far as relative tenderness. If you know that a beef chuck roast is a good candidate for pot-roasting because it is a relatively tough cut, you also know that cuts from the venison shoulder—also known as the chuck—are also best when cooked with methods that tenderize.

The front leg of a deer doesn't have a lot of meat on it. The primary cuts you'll get when you bone it out are a chuck roast, the so-called "chuck tender" and the shank meat.

Place the front leg on your cutting board with the flat side down. Run your fingers over the top side until you locate a ridge of bone that runs from the edge of the shoulder towards the "elbow." Note that the ridge isn't in the center of the shoulder; one portion is much larger than the other. Your first cuts will be along the ridge, on the wider side.

Cut down along the ridge until your knife hits the blade bone; then, turn your knife sideways and scrape/cut along the blade, pulling the meat away with your other hand (photo H). When you reach the edge of the blade, turn the leg over and continue cutting the meat away from the back side, until you have cut away the large shoulder roast.

The small cut on the other side of the ridge is a neat-looking muscle that's called the chuck tender. This name is a misnomer, because this piece is not tender at all. I like to make jerky with the chuck tender, since the muscle is lean and straight with no silverskin or other connective tissues running through it. Cut this muscle away from the bone, just as you did the shoulder roast (photo I).

All that's left of the shoulder is the shank. As with beef or lamb shank, this cut is filled with tendons and tough connective tissue. Best cooking methods are lengthy stewing, as is often done with lamb shanks; grinding for sausage or burger; or for venison stock. If you choose to bone out this meat, be prepared for a long session of tedious scraping, to remove all the connective tissue and tendons.

The large boneless shoulder roast you've cut can be tied up with heavy kitchen twine for pot roasting; you may get two or three roasts out of it if the animal is large. This meat is also excellent for stew. Remember, since meat from the shoulder is tough, you can't use it for regular roasting; it needs long, slow cooking to tenderize. Mark wrapped packages as "chuck" so you know how to cook the meat.

Wrapping & Freezing

All boned meat should be wrapped, labeled and frozen as soon as you finish each portion. I wrap each piece tightly with plastic cling-wrap, smoothing the wrap against the meat since pockets of air will cause freezer-burn. The plastic-wrapped meat then gets two or three layers of freezer paper around it; the shiny side of the freezer paper should face in. Seal the package with freezer tape and label each package with a waterproof marker, noting the type and cut of meat and the date (for example, "Deer, boneless shoulder, 10/2000"). Freeze the meat in a single layer as soon as you are done wrapping.

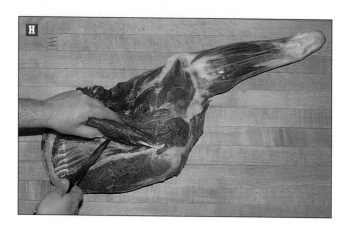

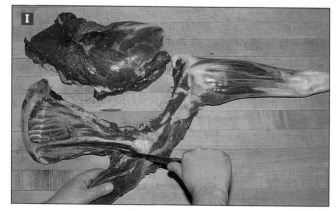

Here's an important tip for cutting and wrapping: even if you're planning to cut the meat into smaller pieces for cooking, freeze large pieces. For example, rather than cutting the shoulder into stew-sized cubes before freezing, wrap and freeze a whole chunk of meat (enough for a meal), then cut it up just before cooking. Larger cuts have less surface exposed to freezer burn and moisture loss, so you'll have juicier meat if you freeze large rather than small cuts.

You will inevitably end up with scraps and small pieces that will eventually be ground or find their way into the stew pot. I keep a gallon-sized freezer-weight zip-top bag handy, and put these pieces into it as I go. When the bag has a pound or two of meat in it, I roll it up, pressing out as much air as possible, then wrap the sealed bag in freezer paper.

Finally, the bones make excellent stock. I keep a large food-safe plastic bag handy, and put the bones into it as I proceed; I keep this bag in the refrigerator or an ice-filled cooler until I am finished.

Butchering the Loins & Ribs

The loins are the next cut that will be ready for final butchering. These boneless strips of meat are easy to finish, since all that's required is trimming away the silverskin and cutting into meal-sized portions. *Silverskin* is a tough, silvery connective tissue that's found between muscle groups throughout all animals. A flexible fillet knife works best for removing silverskin. Place the meat on the cutting board with the silverskin down. Slice through the meat just to the silverskin, then turn your knife sideways and cut/scrape along the silverskin (photo J). If you've ever skinned a fish fillet, the basic technique is exactly the same. As you cut the loin away from the

silverskin, cut it into desired portion sizes; again, even if you plan to make steaks later, freeze the meat in a large piece and steak it later, to prevent moisture loss. Wrap, label and freeze the loin.

If you're saving the ribs rather than boning out the meat between them, you'll need to remove the sternum and ridge of cartilage from the bottom of the ribs (photo K). A good stout knife works best

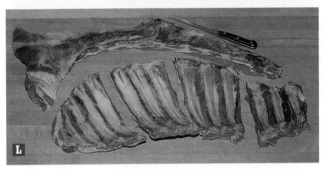

for this, as you'll be cutting through some fairly hard cartilage joints; be very careful to avoid cutting yourself as you do this. You may need to clean up some blood-shot tissue from the outside of the ribs, since a heart-lung shot will have damaged some of this meat (always trim and discard blood-shot meat before wrapping and freezing).

Cut the ribs into three- or four-bone portions (photo L). Then, stack the ribs on top of one another, making a nice, compact bundle. Wrap in several layers of plastic wrap, then overwrap with several layers of foil, smoothing the foil against the contour of the ribs. Circle the foil-wrapped ribs with freezer tape, to keep everything together, then label the freezer tape and freeze the ribs.

If you aren't a rib fan, simply cut the meat from between the ribs, discarding fat or connective tissue, and put the meat with your "to be ground" batch.

Continued …

Boning the Hindquarters

The top part of the hind leg—also called the ham—contains four major muscle groups. The names used

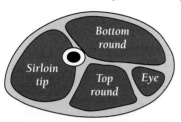

for these venison cuts are the same as those used for comparable beef cuts: sirloin tip, top round, bottom round and eye of round. All large animals have basically the same muscle structure; if you look at a ham steak, you'll see the various cuts.

Place the hind leg on your cutting board, and locate the football-shaped sirloin tip at the front of the leg. There's a natural seam between the sirloin

tip and the top round; locate this and begin working the muscles apart at this seam, using your fingers (photo M). Use your boning knife to cut the connective tissue (photo N), and continue pulling and cutting until you have separated the top round and eye of round from the rest of the hind leg (photo O).

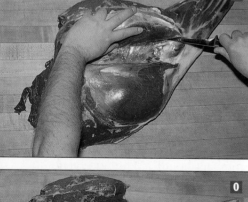

Now begin cutting along the main leg bone to free the sirloin tip. Continue cutting and scraping as close to the bone as

possible (photo P), until you have removed the sirloin tip and any rump meat attached to it.

The bottom round is now the only major muscle that's still attached to the bone. Continue cutting against the bone (photo Q) until the bottom round is free. You'll notice a long, putty-colored gland attached to the bottom round; trim this away carefully and discard it.

As with the front leg, you're left with a bone and shank, in addition to the boneless roasts (photo R). Meat from the ham is fairly tender, so it works well for

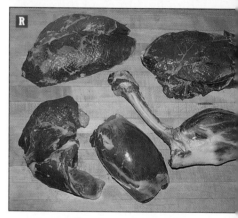

roasting. You may want to butterfly the top round, which is rather flat, then stuff and roll it. The eye of round on deer or antelope is a bit small to use as a roast, but works well for stroganoff, stir-fry dishes and the like. On elk or moose, however, the eye of round is large enough to make a fine roast. Trim off any silverskin or fat before wrapping and freezing your roasts.

Follow these steps carefully to butcher your own deer, and I can just about guarantee you will never take one to a processor again!

Teresa Marrone
Minneapolis, MN

European Head Mount

You've just bagged a nice head ... not a trophy, but not small, either, and you want to do something special with it. It isn't worth the expense of a head or shoulder mount, but you don't just want to whack off the antlers and hang them in the garage. The solution is the European mount.

You have seen these mounts in pictures, movies and possibly in some sporting goods stores. It's the mount with the antlers on top of a white skull. This mount is easy to do at home; all you need is a pot big enough to boil the head in, some detergent, a bottle of bleach and a knife.

There are many variations to this type of mount, but here is the formula that I've found works best. First, I bring a pot full of water to a boil. While the water is warming up, I skin the hide off the skull and trim it a little. Then I add a cup of Biz detergent to the water and put the head in. *Don't boil it for too long!* Ten to 15 minutes is about right; don't go beyond 20 minutes. If the skull is boiled too long, the bones will soften, causing the teeth to fall out and possibly making the skull fall apart.

Take the boiled head out and scrape off as much of the meat as possible. Add more detergent to the water and boil the head for 15 minutes longer. Take it out and scrape some more; repeat this process until all the meat and gristle have been removed. I change the water between each boiling, but it probably isn't necessary.

To remove the brains and also give you a flat base for mounting,

cut the back of the head off with a saw. As an alternate technique, if you wish to display the finished head on a table rather than on the wall or on a plaque, leave the skull intact and use a bent coat hanger to remove the brains through the hole in the back of the skull.

After the skull is cleaned, fill the pot with clean water, heat to boiling and then add a gallon of bleach. Put the skull in it and boil for about ten minutes, then remove it and let it dry.

A note of caution: the bones may become very brittle after this process. Once I dropped a skull I had worked on, and the nose bones shattered into a million pieces. But if you're careful with the mount, you'll have a unique and beautiful display piece.

Jerry Rustad
Kemmerer, WY

TOP: *Boiling the skull outside will help minimize odors in the house. Note that the rack is not in the water, just the head.*

ABOVE: *The finished European mount, ready to be placed on a plaque or the wall.*

Don't Waste Big Game Meat

Being a full-time meat cutter and a part-time taxidermist, I've seen a lot of spoiled game—meat that could easily have been salvaged, and capes that can't be mounted due to incorrect handling after the kill. These tips will help prevent this waste from happening.

- When first approaching an animal that you have shot, determine if it's dead or still alive. If it's been more than 30 seconds since the animal died, don't cut the throat; its heart has long since quit pumping. The cup or so of blood that you will let isn't going to make the meat taste any better. Many a cape has been ruined this way.
- When dressing an animal that you'll have to drag a long way,

make the abdominal evisceration as small as possible. The smaller the hole, the less chance dirt has to enter the body cavity.
- After you hang the animal, wash the inside of the rib cage with vinegar. This will kill any bacteria lurking around. A little vinegar will also make short work of any blood shot.
- After the animal has been hung, skinned and bagged, sprinkle black pepper on the meat where the bag is tied off. This will keep flies and yellowjackets from landing.

Jeremy Evers
Burns, OR

Drag Deer Without Snagging

Have you ever watched a buck going through thick brush? The buck lays its head back so its rack is right against the shoulders. You can use this information to help you on your next deer drag. Here's what I do.

Before I head out hunting, I stop by my farmer friend's house and ask for a few pieces of bale twine to put in my pocket. When I get my deer dressed out, I cut a slit in the lower jaw, alongside the tongue; then I slip the bale twine through the slit and over the deer's nose. (If you're planning to mount the head, slip a handkerchief between the twine and the nose to avoid cuts.)

Next, cut a stick about a foot long. Make a loop at the other end of the twine and slip the stick through the loop. Now you and your buddy can each grab one end of the stick and head down the trail. The buck's antlers will lay back against the shoulders, and seldom snag. If you're dragging without a partner, loop another piece of twine to the first, put it behind your neck and under your arms; now your hands are free to carry your gun.

Clifton Nygaard
Hawick, MN

Easy Ruffed Grouse Dressing

Ruffed grouse are easy to field dress. Place the grouse on its back, then place your feet on the wing bones, snugged right up against the body. Grasp the legs in your hands and pull steadily up toward your waist. The head and innards will remain attached to the spine, leaving you with the breast attached to the wings. The breast meat cools more quickly this way than if the bird is left whole. Remove the wings when you are finished with the hunt, or when it is legal to do so.

David Zembiec
Adams, NY

THE EXPERT'S NOTEBOOK

Don't Overcook Waterfowl ...
by Chris Winchester

For those old-time waterfowlers who do not enjoy the taste of ducks and geese, I dare to say that they have been overcooking the birds.

There is nothing more delicious than teal breast cooked on a hot grill until rare to medium-rare. The same holds true for other ducks and geese as well: waterfowl, especially the delicious breast meat, is best when cooked to medium-rare at most. This may be too radical of a culinary departure for some, but for those looking for a delicious way to eat waterfowl, you owe it to yourself, and to your game, to try this method.

quick tip

Don't Split Deer Between the Hams

Rather than splitting the pelvic bone between the hams, I use the reaming method when dressing big game. I prefer this for several reasons. One, it's easier to drag an animal when the hind legs aren't flopping apart all over the place. And more importantly, since I haven't cut between the hams (exposing this delicious meat to air and dirt) I don't have to trim away any dried or damaged meat from the ham area when I'm boning the animal.

Teresa Marrone
Minneapolis, MN

Index

A

Acorns
    as game forage, 38, 39, 107
    making acorn scent, 86
Aim point, 104, 114
Ambushing
    pronghorn, 36, 37, 101, 102
    turkeys, 46
    whitetails, 74, 107, 112
    see also: Stands & stand hunting
Antelope, see Pronghorn
Antlers
    European head mount, 153
    for rattling, 95, 119
    preparing trophy antlers for
        airline shipment, 90
    rattling technique, 89, 119, 121
Archery hunting
    and stand placement, 88
    archery advantage, 74
    arrow weight, 76
    clothing, 87, 113
    decoying, 102, 103
    elk, 78, 79
    equipment, 68, 87, 98
    minimizing noise, 76, 77
    practicing, 114
    pronghorn, 12, 13, 102, 103
    shot placement, 114
    stalking, 65
    turkeys, 42
    whitetails, 58-60, 68, 74, 107,
        121
    wind indicator, 76, 77
Armguard, 87
Arrow weight, 76
    see also: Archery hunting
ATV to carry equipment, 105

B

Backpack hunting, 93, 111, 128
Back rest, 106
Barometric pressure, 127
Barrel, breaking in, 79

Base camp
    hunting away from, 10
Bears
    baiting, 28, 32, 47
    behavior, 18, 22, 48
    hunting pressure, 10, 16
    hunting techniques & equip-
        ment, 16, 18, 22-24, 28, 32, 39,
        48-51, 115
    locations & habitat, 16, 22, 23
    tracking, 106
Beds & bedding behavior
    hunting near, 74, 88, 106
    locating bedded game, 27
    pigs, 15, 39, 71
    pronghorn, 13
    whitetails, 38, 107
Binoculars
    carrying in field, 137
    choosing, 108
    general use tips, 11, 115
    shooting sticks for, 115
    See also: Spot-and-stalk hunting
Bleat call, 20, 121
Blinds & blind hunting
    adding confidence decoy, 47
    approaching, 113
    camo netting for blind, 109
    for bears, 48
    for predators, 85
    for pronghorn, 12, 102, 103
    for turkeys, 25, 42, 109
    for waterfowl, 93, 110
    for whitetails, 40, 112
Blood trail, 71, 84, 106, 142
Blueberries, 135
Boars, see: Pigs
Boats in cold weather, 104
Boning big game, 148-152
Boone and Crockett Club, 16, 55
Boots
    camouflage, 26
    field repair, 90
    recommendations, 97, 98, 113,
        119, 125
Box call, 46, 51, 54
    see also: Calling, Turkeys
Buckshot, patterning, 76
Butchering big game at home,
    148-151

C

Calling
    deer, 35, 51, 89, 121
    ducks, 31
    elk, 78, 120
    geese, 47
    grunt call, 35, 40, 68, 89, 96,
        97, 109
    keeping calls dry, 51
    pronghorn, 20, 103
    turkeys, 25, 42, 46, 51, 54, 61
Camouflage
    animals' natural camouflage, 30
    clothing, 26, 84, 85, 88, 89, 93,
        104, 119
    concealing blinds & stands, 93,
        109
    face & body, 84, 93, 99
    head net, 113
    netting for blind, 109
    tape, 109
Camps & camping
    campfire starting, 132, 136
    equipment & tips, 90, 106, 137
    food, 135, 145, 149
    location, 10, 128
    sleeping pad, 111
Canada geese, 44
    see also: Geese
Canvasbacks, 75
    see also: Ducks
Caping deer, 140
Caribou, 10
Chest guard, 87
Choke recommendations, 69, 75
Chukar, 75
Cleaning guns, 69, 81
Climbing treestands, 58-60, 89
Clothing & related gear
    camouflage, 26, 84, 85, 88, 89,
        93, 104, 119
    for cold weather, 86, 93, 104,
        105, 109, 125
Cold weather
    and archery, 87
    and waterfowl hunting, 53, 95,
        104
    boat care, 104
    camping, 111
    clothing & related gear, 86, 93,
        104, 105, 109, 125

gun tip, 135
safety, 134
specialty equipment, 92
water supply, 111
Comfort
    on stand or in blind, 46, 109,
        111, 125
    while waterfowl hunting, 104,
        125
Cooking
    ruffed grouse, 145
    waterfowl, 155
    woodcock, 31
Cottontails, see: Rabbits
Coues' deer, 16
Cover
    deer hiding in, 11
    glassing edges, 11

D

Decoys & decoy hunting
    adding motion to, 110
    cold weather, 53, 95, 104
    confidence decoys, 47, 94
    for deer, 52
    for predators, 85
    for pronghorn, 12, 102, 103
    for turkeys, 25, 42, 46
    for waterfowl, 44, 47, 53, 91,
        93, 104, 110
    making goose decoy chair,
        116-117
    repairing, 94
    retrieving, 95, 104
    uses for old decoys, 94
Deer, see: Coues' deer, Mule deer,
    Sitka black-tailed deer,
    Whitetails
Distance, judging, 70, 95, 103
Dogs
    field care, 127
    grouse hunting, 14
    pheasant hunting, 53, 75
    pig hunting, 39
    raccoon hunting, 63
    woodcock hunting, 30, 31
Downhill shooting, 27
Dragging deer, 154, 155
Driving
    deer, 8, 37, 43, 45
    escape points, 45
    hunting pressure to drive game, 32

one-man, 43
pheasants, 53, 57
to figure out pattern, 21
Ducks
    behavior, 93
    calling, 31
    camouflage, 84, 93
    cooking, 155
    decoying, 44, 95, 104
    dressing & plucking, 144
    hunting techniques & equip-
        ment, 44, 53
    senses, 93
    shotguns & shells for, 75

E

Elk
    behavior, 20
    butchering, 152
    calling, 78, 120
    hunting techniques & equip-
        ment, 9, 20, 29, 32, 58, 72,
        73, 78, 120
    locations & habitat, 17, 20,
        29, 58
    non-typical, 73
    quartering & field care, 141- 143
Escape routes & patterns, 21, 32,
    37, 45
Estrus period
    and buck behavior, 9

F

Feeding call, 31
Fences
    hunting along, 102
    sign on, 39
Field dressing
    big game, 141, 142, 145, 154,
        155
    birds, 144, 155
    kit for, 140
    quartering elk, 141
Field judging game, 52, 70, 108
Fire starting, 132, 136
Flagging for pronghorn, 103
Flushing
    grouse, 71
    pheasants, 53, 57, 75
    rabbits, 26
    woodcock, 30, 31
Foods & feeding

bears, 22
game locations near feeding
    area, 17, 26, 46, 71
hunting near feeding area, 8, 25,
    39, 46, 47, 74
importance to game, 19, 38
improving habitat for, 19
pigs, 15, 39
pronghorn, 12
waterfowl, 93
whitetails, 38, 74, 127
wilderness food, 135
woodcock, 30, 31
Footwear, see: Boots
Fox
    as predator of gamebirds, 53
    following up missed shot, 12
    fox call to attract pronghorn, 103
    fox urine cover scent, 85
Freezing game
    game birds, 144
    big game, 148, 150, 151
Friction calls, 51
    see also: Calling, Turkeys
Fuzz sticks, 132

G

Geese
    calling, 47
    camouflage, 84, 104
    cooking, 155
    decoying, 44, 95, 104
    dressing & plucking, 144
    hunting techniques & equip-
        ment, 44, 47, 116-117
    making goose decoy chair,
        116-117
    senses, 47
    shotguns & shells for, 53, 75
Generator, 137
Glassing
    at various distances, 11
    before hunting, 27, 45, 55, 64
    edges of cover, 11
    optics for, 108
    tips, 115, 128
    using shooting sticks, 115
    see also: Binoculars
Gloves
    for cold weather, 86, 104, 105
    for field dressing, 140, 145
Glowsticks, 84

Goats
    behavior & locations, 18
    hunting equipment, 99
    hunting pressure, 10
    spike camps for, 10
Grouse, 75
    see also: Ruffed Grouse
Grunt call, 35, 40, 68, 89, 96, 97, 109
Guns, cleaning, 69, 81
    see also: Muzzleloaders, Rifles, Shotguns & shells

H
Hand signals, 53, 136
Hands, keeping warm, 86, 104, 105
Hanging big game, 148, 154
Hares, 54
Hawk whistle, 53
Head lamp, 111
Hearing protection, 134
Hogs, see: Pigs
Honey burn for bear attractant, 28
Hunting pressure
    and hunt quality, 10, 74
    and seasons, 18, 74
    figuring out pattern, 21
    game activity & locations, 10, 11, 17, 21, 37, 74
    game movement, 20, 37
    taking advantage of, 20, 32
Hydration system, 111
Hypothermia, 134

K
Knot diagrams, 129

L
Late season hunting
    general advice, 18
    pheasants, 75
    waterfowl, 44, 75
    whitetails, 74
Limb Savers, 76

M
Mallards, 44, 75, 93
    see also: Ducks
Meat
    boning big game at home, 148-152
    field care, 143, 145, 154

transporting, 73, 90
Migration by woodcock, 31
Mittens, 86, 105
Moose
    butchering, 152
    hunting pressure, 10, 17
    hunting techniques & equipment, 98
Mountain goats, see: Goats
Mounts
    European head mount, 153
    turkey mount, 146, 147
Muffs, 105
Mule deer,
    behavior, 55, 62, 70
    hunting techniques & equipment, 45, 52, 55, 56, 58, 62, 63, 91
    locations & habitat, 55, 58
Muzzleloaders
    accessories, 80, 98, 99
    for bears, 48-51
    for pronghorn, 100-104
    for whitetails, 96, 97
    general advice, 77, 80
    wet weather hunting, 80

N
Noise made by hunters
    controlling, 64
    deliberately making noise, 43, 54, 64
    minimizing, 76, 77, 80, 111
    noisy equipment, 58
    talking, 53

O
Open habitat & pronghorn, 12, 100
Outfitters
    talking with, 18, 19
    working with, 63, 135

P
Packing out meat, 10
Partridge, 75
    see also: Ruffed Grouse
Patterning game
    general tips, 91, 126
    mule deer, 91
    pigs, 15 , 91
    pronghorn, 65
    turkeys, 42, 44

whitetails, 21, 38, 74
Patterning shotgun, 76
Peroxide to follow blood trail, 106
Pheasants
    behavior, 53
    driving, 53, 57
    shotguns & shells, 69, 75
Photos
    aerial photos, 17, 91
    avoiding green eyes, 130
    tips for taking, 128, 131
Physical condition & hunting, 18, 22, 24
Pigs
    behavior, 15, 39, 71
    hunting techniques & equipment, 15, 39, 90
Pintails, 75
    see also: Ducks
Plucking
    grouse, 145
    waterfowl, 144
Pope and Young Club, 12, 55
Portable treestands, 89
Predator calls,
    over-using, 31
    to lure pronghorn, 103
Predator hunting, 31, 85, 104
Processing big game
    boning big game at home, 148-152
    taking meat to processor, 143
Pronghorn
    behavior, 12, 13, 36, 37, 100, 101-103
    butchering, 152
    calling, 20, 103
    field judging, 52
    hunting techniques & equipment, 9, 12, 13, 20, 36, 37, 52, 65, 100-104, 108
    locations & habitat, 12, 100
    senses, 13, 65, 100
    speed, 100
Public land, 16-18, 45, 55, 71

Q
Quail, 75
Quartering big game, 141, 143

R

Rabbits
    behavior, 127
    habitat & locations, 26
Raccoons, 63
Rain
    and game activity, 18, 46
    hunting in, 51, 80, 90
    raingear, 98, 119
Rangefinders, 70, 95
Rattling
    and stand height, 89
    antlers for, 95, 119
    tips & techniques, 119, 121
Ridgetop hunting, 27
Rifles
    accessories, 98
    and stand placement, 88
    breaking in barrel, 79
    cleaning, 69, 81
    stainless steel barrels, 72, 73
Rubs & rub lines
    hunting near, 74
    making mock rubs, 107
    pig rubs, 39
    scouting, 8, 38, 39
Ruffed grouse
    and weather, 14, 127
    cooking, 145
    dressing, 155
    hunting techniques, 14, 71
    shotguns & shells, 75

S

Safety
    and weather, 135
    hunting dangerous game, 39
    treestand safety, 58, 60, 88, 124
Scent
    apple scent, 118
    attractant scent, 35, 112, 115
    bird scent & dogs, 14
    controlling, 96, 107, 113
    cover scent, 35-37, 44, 85
    dispersing scent, 92, 96, 108,
        112, 118
    human scent & game animals,
        13, 22, 24, 44, 50, 55, 58, 64,
        78, 88, 96
    making acorn scent, 86
    scent-blocking products, 96,
        113, 124

scent line, 112
Scouting
    geese, 47
    general tips, 8, 14, 55, 61, 71
    in-season, 38
    post-season, 38
    preseason, 21, 61, 101, 102
    what to look for, 8, 39
    with telephone, 61
Scope
    general usage advice, 80, 108
    to judge game, 70
Scrapes
    hunting near, 74
    making mock scrape, 97, 115
    scouting, 8, 38
Senses of game
    deer, 44, 58, 113
    ducks, 93
    geese, 47
    pronghorn, 13, 65, 100
    turkeys, 42
Sheep
    hunting pressure, 10
    hunting equipment, 108
    spike camps for, 10
Shooting sticks & rests, 70, 90, 104,
    106, 115
Shooting technique, 70, 80
Shotguns & shells
    and stand placement, 88
    choke recommendations, 69, 75
    choosing, 75
    cleaning, 69
    for upland birds, 69, 75
    for waterfowl, 53, 75
    for woodcock, 31, 75
    patterning, 76
Shot placement, 104, 114
Silencers for bow, 76
Sitka black-tailed deer, 17
Skinning game
    big game, 143
    skinning turkey for mount, 146
Slate call, 51
    see also: Calling, Turkeys
Slingshot, 43, 106
Smell
    sense of in deer, 44
    sense of in pronghorn, 13
Snow geese, 104
    see also: Geese

Snowshoe hares, 54
Spike camps, 10, 18, 22
Spot-and-stalk hunting
    for fox, 12
    for pigs, 39
    for pronghorn, 12, 13, 20
    hand signals, 136
    See also Stalking
Spotting scope, 12, 55
    see also: Spot-and-stalk hunting
Stalking
    deer, 57
    elk, 78
    general advice, 65, 70, 80, 95,
        111
    pronghorn, 12, 13, 20, 100, 101
    see also Spot-and-stalk hunting
Stands & stand hunting
    adding confidence decoy, 47
    and wind, 44, 88
    approaching, 51, 64, 112, 113
    baiting, 28, 32
    climbing stands, 58-60, 89
    comfort, 46, 111, 125
    decoys near, 42, 47
    for pigs, 39
    for predators, 85
    for pronghorn, 12, 102
    for turkeys, 42
    for whitetails, 58-60, 91, 96, 97,
        106, 107, 112, 121
    getting weapon into stand, 121
    location & placement, 38, 39,
        44, 85, 88, 89, 91
    path to, 96, 112
    portable, 58, 59, 89
    position in tree, 88, 89
    rattling from, 121
    safety, 58, 60, 88, 89, 124
    scent control, 107, 113
    scent use, 32, 58, 92, 96, 1
        12, 118
    scouting locations, 38
    shooting from, 76, 88, 114
    stand height, 88, 89
    usage tips, 76, 87-88, 91, 102
Still-hunting
    deer, 44, 51, 55
    general advice, 57
Storms
    and game activity, 127
    see also: Weather

Success ratios
    and hunting pressure, 10
    interpreting, 19

T

Tagging game, 90, 92, 142
Taxidermy
    caring for game, 140
    European head mount, 153
    turkey mount, 146, 147
Teal, 75
    see also: Ducks
Topographical maps, 17, 43, 92
Tracks
    determining when tracks were
       made, 29
    scouting for, 8
Trails
    following blood trail, 71, 84,
       106, 142
    game activities on trails, 15
    game trails, 19
    hunting trails & paths, 14, 112
    scouting, 8
Transporting meat, 73, 90
Treestands, see: Stands & stand
    hunting
Trophy hunting
    and late season, 18
    behavior of trophy game, 39
    field judging, 52
    locations, 16-18, 55
    optics for, 108
    preparing trophy antlers for
       airline shipment, 90
    taxidermy tips, 140
    tips, 19, 55, 62, 63
Turkeys
    behavior, 42, 46, 54
    calling, 25, 42, 46, 51, 54, 61
    clothing, 26
    hunting techniques & equip-
       ment, 25, 42, 46, 51, 54,
       61, 106
    locations & habitat, 42
    mounting, 146, 147
    photographing, 131
    senses, 42
Turkey vest, 109

U

Upland birds
    dressing, 144
    shotguns & shells, 69, 75
    see also specific upland birds

V

Vest, 109
Vision
    of ducks, 93
    of pronghorn, 13, 65, 100

W

Water
    and camping, 10
    boiling spring water, 145
    carrying during hunt, 111, 140
    for hunting dog, 127
    hunting near water source, 8,
       15, 36, 47, 65, 101
    importance to game, 19, 31,
       36-39, 71, 101
    protecting ammo from, 53
    surviving in cold water, 134
Waterfowl, see: Ducks, Geese
Waxing waterfowl, 144
Weather
    and game activities, 18, 31, 39,
       46, 48, 127
    and game care, 140
    and pronghorn hunting, 12
    and travel, 135
    cold weather boat care, 104
    cold weather gun tip, 135
    hunting gear, 86, 87, 92, 98,
       104, 105, 111, 119, 125, 137
    see also: Rain, Storms, Wind
Whitetails
    behavior, 9, 11, 14, 21, 35, 37,
       38, 45, 51, 57,58, 76, 89, 91,
       96, 113, 127
    boning big game at home,
       148-152
    calling, 35, 51, 89, 121
    hunting techniques & equip-
       ment, 9, 14, 33, 35, 37, 43,
       45, 57, 58, 74, 76, 84, 87, 88,
       89, 96, 97, 106, 108, 112,
       113, 115, 118, 119, 121
    improving habitat for, 19
    locations & habitat, 14, 19
    senses, 44, 58, 113

Wind
    and calling, 20, 25
    and camp location, 128
    and scent, 13, 96
    calculating wind adjustment, 126
    caribou movements, 18
    general hunting advice, 44
    grouse hunting, 14
    mule deer hunting, 62
    pig hunting, 71
    predator hunting, 85
    pronghorn hunting, 13
    stand placement, 88, 112, 113
    turkey movements & hunting,
       25, 42, 46
    wind indicator, 77, 107, 137
Woodcock
    about, 30, 31
    shotguns & shells, 31, 75
Wood ducks, 75
    see also: Ducks